What people are saying about this publication

Michael J O'Connor, Assistant Head of School, Technological University Dublin, School of Culinary Arts & Food Technology City Campus, Dublin. Congrats Jimmy on this **magnificent publication**. We at TU Dublin, School of Culinary Arts and Food Technology are honoured to have your skills, expertise and passion.... !!!

Thomas Johann Biesewig, Brand Ambassador - South-East Asia at Steinmetz Premium Flour, Hamburg, Germany .Downloaded the eBook already. **It's a masterpiece**. I never saw a better book about lamination dough.

247 baker, Verified Purchase Amazon.com 29/06/2020 **Incredible book on Lamination**. I just bought this book and I have to say it's fantastic. Chef and Author Jimmy Griffin is an amazing person, who is gifted in teaching the art of viennoiserie. He explains the different folding techniques used in each process and clearly explains the resulting eating qualities from using the various folds. He has numerous videos uploaded to YouTube which help explain his methods. I have never met the man, but I have followed him on Instagram for years. I have to say, I am in awe of him. Not only did he once get attacked by a conger eel, but he also broke his back. His resilience and passion for his craft is evident in his book. I have taken lamination courses from Chef Peter Yuen, Chef Hans Ovando and other chefs throughout the years. Chef Griffin's book is just as incredible as their courses. I highly recommend buying his book. I am looking forward to the printed copy once it comes in. You should also follow him on Instagram @jimmyg51.

Vrian Sevilla, Verified Purchase Amazon.com 01/07/2020. **The ultimate book of croissant!** I'm lovin' it! Thank you for this Chef Jimmy! I've been on a scavenger hunt for this kind of book for a long time. There is no other book that covers every process in the production of croissant than this. Every step of the process is explained. I'm a happy camper!

John Bickerstaff, Verified Purchase Amazon.com 28/06/2020

A must for any serious baker. Amazing history, background, technically! This book covers all of it, along with multiple hints, suggestions on flavours and skills. A must for any serious baker.

Published by
Jimmy Griffin Publications
Wild Winds, Forramoyle West
Barna, Co Galway
Ireland. H91 XHY7

First edition June 2020

ISBN - 978-1-8381082-2-9

Citation:

Griffin, J. (2020). The Art of Lamination, Advanced Technical Laminated Pastry Production 2020. 1st ed. Galway, Ireland: Jimmy Griffin Publications.

Table of Contents

Table of Figures

List of Tables

Glossary of terms and abbreviations

Beurrage	Preparation/plasticising butter prior to lamination
CDM	Coupe du Monde de la Boulangerie – World Cup of Bakery
CDMC	Coupe du Monde Chocolatine – World Cup of Chocolatine
Core temperature	The temperature at the centre or core of a pastry/block of pastry
DDT	Desired Dough Temperature
DTP	Dough Touching Points
IR	Infrared thermometer
Lamination number	A number given to the number of folds given to the pastry
Lock-in	Placing butter between layers of dough to begin the lamination process
RH	Relative Humidity
RT	Room Temperature
Sheeting	Rolling pastry out thin to fold or cut
WT	Water Temperature

The classic sourdough croissant 5-4-3

Foreword

Making high quality laminated yeasted pastry requires many capabilities: knowledge, skill, understanding, technical ability, procedure, precision, patience and practice, among other things. Passion is the greatest of all of these. The reward for producing excellent pastry is the satisfaction it brings not only to its creator but also to the consumers who delight in this creation time and time again. I hope to stimulate your creativity with the photos and techniques in my book; to give you lots of ideas to create, to imagine and the knowledge to execute these ideas for your own creations.

Jimmy Griffin, President, Coupe Du Monde de la Boulangerie/World Cup of Baking, Paris 2016.

Dedications

I dedicate this book firstly to my beloved family, my wife Bogna, son Dillon and daughters Janice and Sophie. I love you all very much, and I could not have finished this book without your support. 2020 saw a terrible disease, Covid-19 sweep across the world changing the lives of many millions of people. Many mourners have been left behind. It was also the year that my friend, colleague and mentor at Technological University Dublin, Diarmuid Murphy parted this world and left us for another, hopefully, brighter place. Diarmuid was one of my lecturers when I studied for my MSc. He brought joy, brightness, humour and interest to all his classes, and he was a significant inspiration in my life, prompting me in my appreciation, writing, reading and research in bakery. Diarmuid also loved my croissants and pastry. This book is for you Diarmuid.

Influences in my professional life

There are so many people who I am thankful to, and I would have to write another book to mention them all. I wish to thank my global bakery family, whose friendships have endured and whose influences live on in me through creativity and passion. Derek O' Brien, my friend and mentor, retired Head of the National Bakery School Kevin Street, Dublin; retired Head of Diploma in German Baking course at Akademie Deutsches Bäckerhandwerk Weinheim, Germany and Director of the Baking Academy of Ireland, Dublin. My former Irish bakery team colleagues over the years: Tommy, Frank, Paul, Gemma, Robert, Michelle and Dolores. Dr Frank Cullen, who has always fully supported me in my work at TU Dublin as a lecturer and inspires me to write and think academically. Finally, my dear friend Christian Vabret, creator of Coupe du Monde de la Boulangerie who has believed in me and honoured me with my appointment of being a juror at the world events for nearly two decades. Christian made it possible for me to meet, watch, observe and learn from the world's best bakers. Many thanks to you all.

About the author

James, or Jimmy Griffin as he is more popularly known, is a sixth-generation master baker from Galway Ireland. He has forty years' experience in the bakery industry, growing up in the family business. He is a specialist in viennoiserie, sourdough, bread and cake production. He holds a Master's degree in Food Product Development and Culinary Innovation and lectures to honours degree bakery students at the School of Culinary Arts and Food Technology, Technological University, Cathal Brugha Street, Dublin. He also works as an advisor and consultant to industry. Jimmy grew up being competitive and as an apprentice, won many national bakery competitions. Later in his career, he represented Ireland and competed in the European Championships as the viennoiserie candidate three times; winning bronze at the Coupe D' Europe de la Boulangerie 1997. He went on to coach the very successful Irish bakery team from 2002 until 2005. Jimmy has also been an international bakery jury member since 2001 for most of the world championships and world master's competitions, the bakery Olympics of the industry. In 2016, Jimmy was appointed as president of the Jury at the Coupe du Monde de la Boulangerie in Paris. He regularly lectures and teaches overseas and has been involved with baking and competitions in most continents of the world. In 2015, he was also honoured by his Russian colleagues and awarded an Honorary Professorship of Stavropol University in Russia. In May 2019, he came out of competitive retirement to compete in the Coupe du Monde Chocolatine in Toulouse, France, taking the silver medal for his creations in hand-laminated pastry at the event. He is very active on social media platforms, and regularly updates his pages with exciting recipes, procedures, and products. Married to his wife Bogna, Jimmy has three children, Dillon (23), Janice (22) and Sophie (14) (2020). In addition to his test baking passion, Jimmy is a licenced fixed-wing pilot; an aerobatic pilot; seaplane pilot, judo blackbelt instructor, divemaster and a former marathon runner. He enjoys writing and his honours degree dissertation titled "An investigative study into the beneficial use of seaweed in bread and the broader food industry" has been viewed and downloaded over 6000 times. He is currently finishing a book featuring internationally acclaimed bakers' recipes, a book on the history of the family bakery titled Fully Baked, and another book on Panettone and Levito Madre. Jimmy had two brothers, Mark lives with his family in London and David, formerly in Malta. Sadly, while finishing this publication, David died suddenly aged 57 years. We will always remember him in our hearts and our minds. Sleep in peace David.

Honorary Professor of Bakery and Pastry Arts, Stavropol University, Russia 2015

With Janice and Bogna Griffin

Abstract

Internationally, there are as many terms for the folds and type of folds used when laminating pastry as there are languages. In the USA, they refer to letter fold, envelope, double fold, in Ireland and the UK it is a book fold, a half-fold a single fold, fold-over etc.…Then to add further confusion, pastry can be described as being made by the English method, the French method, blitz method, inverse butter method, Dutch method, German method and the Scotch method! It can all become very baffling, especially when translated into a dozen different languages. There is one common denominator; however, that encompasses all this process, and that is a numerical solution to the language barriers. Many of the top bakers in the world now communicate lamination techniques by describing the folds as a number instead of a name. My colleague Peter Yuen, a noted world lamination specialist has also taught this system worldwide. This system is truly international, and, in this paper, I explain in detail the correct use of this numbering system.

Additionally, having reviewed countless textbooks on the subject, my experience in teaching and jury work seeks out many of the gaps in the education of viennoiserie to practitioners of the white art. This work provides both a scientific and a straightforward explanation of many of the finer points of producing great laminated pastry.

A brief history of the croissant from 17th century

The birth of the croissant was a series of evolutionary steps which began with the kipferl form, shared in Austria and Germanic baking at the time and the invention of flaky, laminated pastry. The first recognised puff pastry recipe or *pâte feuilletée* was documented in François Pierre de la Varenne's 1653 book, *Le Pâtissier François*. This iconic historical cookbook was the first to record recipes and methods of the French pastry arts (Goldstein & Mintz, 2015). According to the Culinary Institute of America (CIA) (2016:289). the croissant was first fashioned by the Hungarian bakers of Budapest to signify and celebrate the liberation of their beloved city from the Turkish army in 1686 CIA However, in *August Zang and the French Croissant,* Chevallier (2009) contradicts this CIA version of events and that it was the Austrian bakers in Vienna who were under siege in 1683 by the Turkish invaders who invented the croissant Chevallier, (2009:9). The legend recounts that Viennese bakers in 1683, while at work early in the morning heard the Turkish army digging under the walls of Vienna. They alerted their army commanders, and the Turks were routed. The croissant was created to celebrate the liberation of Vienna. Its shape and the name was consequent of the crescent moon, a symbol of Turkish tyranny. The French and Italian bakers soon followed after their Viennese counterparts and included this crescent pastry as part of their daily mantra. The croissant in its original classical form was very different from today's creation as it was made using puff paste with lard and milk, a laminated dough devoid of yeast.

> *When you have mastered puff pastry, you will find it such a satisfying and splendid accomplishment that you will bless yourself for every moment you spent learning the techniques.* Labensky, Sarah, R; Martel, Priscella, Van Damme, Eddy (2009).

Falling sugar prices toward the end of the seventeenth century enabled the rising wealthy merchant dynasties in the prosperous cities of Vienna and Paris to trade in sugar which was once available exclusively to royalty. Café culture as we know it was born about this time and in Paris, this café culture involved meeting over tea, coffee, and cake to discuss revolutionary ideas against King Louis XIV (Willan, 2016).

Anatomy of a croissant

Croissants are generally made from an isosceles triangle-shaped piece of leavened, laminated pastry and coiled from the base to the tip by the baker. Croissants are available worldwide in curved, crescent shape or straight. They can be hand made by artisans in bakeries and pastry kitchens, or industrially mass-produced, frozen, and distributed across the globe. They are possibly the most globally iconic pastry which conjures up an association with France when seen or spoken about. They are available in different quality standards depending on whether they are laminated with butter, pastry margarine or other fats. The percentage of butter in a croissant is usually 30%. The base of the triangle of pastry is referred to as the base or the foot, and the top is known as the tip. The pastry triangle has two flat sides and three cut edges on the outside of the pastry. When a croissant is rolled up, the outsides edges are visible as "steps", and the number of steps is predetermined by the size and length of the isosceles triangle cut to form them. Additionally, the cut triangle is generally stretched further by hand by the baker, further elongating it and allowing the pastry to have more coils or steps. The croissant should not be stressed too much when forming as it will tear when proofing. The pastry, when stretched for forming, should have a graduated thickness extending from the thinnest part at the base to the thickest part at the tip. The bicolor croissant below was made in Reykjavik, Iceland, while assisting Team Iceland as a tutor in January 2018.

Overview and hacks for laminated pastry making

The laminated pastry is usually made by combining a stiff enriched sweet dough with a sheet or block of butter known as a butter block. The dough and butter should be of roughly the same consistency, which favours the creation of even layer formation when rolled and folded together. While pastry margarine and other hard fats can also be used to achieve lamination, the focus of this publication is the production of laminated pastry using butter. The butter should be hammered with a rolling pin, a technique known as Beurrage in French, to plasticise the butterfat and make it malleable for rolling, and it is then formed into a rectangular block known as a butter block. In the makeup process of the pastry, the dough is sheeted out thinly and folded to surround or encapsulate the butter. When the butter and dough combine, it is referred to as pastry.

Standard laminated pastry making practice generally begins with establishing a sandwich of three layers; two layers of dough top and bottom, with the butter block in the centre; like a slice of cheese between two slices of bread. The pastry is formed by rolling or sheeting the dough and butter together in unison. As the pastry is rolled down to form a thin sheet, a process called sheeting, both the dough and butter layers extend out into a thin rectangle of pastry. The dough and butter layers remain separate and intact, forming long thin alternating layers of dough/butter/dough in this sheet of pastry. Once sheeted to an acceptable thickness, the process of building the number of layers to a desired numerical value is achieved by folding the sheeted pastry into pleats which sit on top of each other like building blocks. The most common folds used in laminated pastry making are a book fold, also known as a 4-fold, and a half fold known as a 3-fold. Every time the pastry is sheeted, folded and re sheeted, additional layers are formed within the pastry. It is these layers when folded and built up within the pastry; which contribute towards the creation of the light eating quality, and volume associated with a laminated pastry product. Both the process and temperature control are essential in successful pastry making, as are the number of layers required for a particular product. Croissant generally requires 25 layers; chocolatine 33 layers and puff paste can have well over 100 layers depending on the number of folds given to the pastry. I have identified 20 separate stages in the process of producing laminated pastry, and these are as follows:

The 20 stages of laminated pastry production and handling

1. Weighing of the raw materials
2. Mixing times and desired dough temperature 25-26°C
3. Preparation of the butter block while mixing the dough
4. Bulk fermentation of the dough (45 minutes)
5. Flattening and chilling of the dough (3-4°C) overnight for cold fermentation
6. Lock-in of the butter into a sandwich between the dough using **3** or **5**-layer lock-in
7. Sheeting #1, reducing the pastry down in thickness to between 3-5mm and 1st fold
8. Resting in chilled storage (-18°C between ice blankets if available)
9. Sheeting #2, reducing the pastry down in thickness to between 5-6mm and 2nd fold
10. Chilling/resting (-18°C between ice blankets if available)
11. Final sheeting generally to a thickness of between 3.5-4.0mm
12. Cutting to size and shape
13. Shaping, forming and traying up
14. Proofing (26-27.5°C @ 80% relative humidity RH) 2-3 hours, Wobble test, visually observe the separation of layers at the end of proof time
15. Egg washing (recipe page 73)
16. Retardation (3°C-RH 80%) if holding overnight for baking the following day
17. Freezing (-18°C) if holding for several days, preferably blast freezing after ¾ proof
18. Baking - temperature and time which will depend on whether you use a convection or deck oven.
19. Cooling on wire racks to prevent the bottoms from becoming soggy
20. Finishing/packing

Yeasts used in laminated pastry making

Saccharomyces Cerevisiae or bakers' yeast as it is commonly known is the yeast bakers use mostly throughout the world. It comes in many different forms, from fresh to dried and yeast reproduces by a process known as budding. The reproduction rate of yeast ensures that it roughly doubles in quantity every 90 minutes (Berry, et al., 2012). In theory, the quantity of yeast present in a dough can double in 90 minutes, but factors such as dough temperature, enrichment levels and pH can have a marked effect on yeast reproduction. Placing a yeasted dough into a fridge, for example, will slow down yeast reproduction and placing the dough in a warm proofer can accelerate yeast reproduction. There are many types of baker's yeast available on the market today. Yeast is available as fresh/compressed, freeze-dried/dehydrated and vacuum packed so that the yeast has a very long shelf life at ambient temperature. My personal choice for pastry making is fresh compressed yeast or if available, osmotolerant fresh yeast, a special yeast sold mainly in Europe to produce Brioche and laminated pastry. It performs much better in the high fat/sugar environment of enriched pastry, giving superior tolerance and gassing performance than regular bakers' yeast. Bakers or fresh yeast is the standard stated in all recipes in this book unless otherwise stated. I use 10g dry/30g compressed yeast, but many people also use 10g dry to 20g compressed yeast in smaller batches. Two general types of dried yeast are popular among home bakers in use today: active dry yeast and instant yeast. It is essential to be aware that active dry yeast needs to be rehydrated, that is dissolved in the dough making water before mixing into the dough to activate it. Dried yeasts may also contain emulsifiers and bread improvers for use in bread machines, so attention to the ingredient list is wise if baking for people with extreme allergies. Always use warm water to dissolve active yeast and stimulate the yeast back to life. The second type of yeast is instant yeast, and this yeast can be mixed straight into the dough without pre hydrating. Both types of dried yeasts can be used interchangeably in laminated pastry formulas, without recipe adjustment. However, care needs to be taken to rehydrate the active dried yeast if you are using it or suffer poor gassing performance. In summary, it is best practice to hydrate all forms yeast before making your dough, the warmth of the water encourages good gassing and fermentation of the dough. Always read and follow the manufacturers recommendations when using dry yeast for best results.

Types of flour used in artisan baking in America and Europe

Calvel's "The Taste of Bread" has an extensive table on page 4 showing protein and ash content of US and French flours (Calvel, 2001). The Extraction Rate is the quantity of flour extracted from each wheat berry during the milling process. The lower the extraction rate of flour, the whiter the flour will be as the flour is removed from the centre of the wheat berry, e.g. T-45 flour. The higher the extraction rate, the more bran and percentage of the wheat berry, e.g. T-150 is a dark brown wholemeal flour of almost 98% extraction.

- ➤ Type 45:   Ash content below 0.50   extraction rate   67-70%
- ➤ Type 55:   Ash content 0.50-0.62   extraction rate   75-78%
- ➤ Type 65:   Ash content 0.62-0.75   extraction rate   78-82%
- ➤ Type 80:   Ash content 0.75-0.90   extraction rate   82-85%
- ➤ Type 110:   Ash content 1.00-1.20   extraction rate   85-90%
- ➤ Type 150:   Ash content above 1.40   extraction rate   90-98%

(Calvel, 2001).

Generally, American flour's ash content is measured based on a 14% flour humidity; the ash content numbers cannot be compared directly. For example, a French flour with a measurement of 0.55 ash (type 55) corresponds to a US 0.46 ash content flour. It is also fair to say that there are no direct equivalent flours between the French/German and US types as many US millers do not list flour ash content on the package. A separate flour specification sheet must be requested to establish the ash content of each individual flour type. The inability to establish like for like equivalents in flour types is mostly due to the difference in milling process steps by each miller. Milling consists of a series of steps of sorting, grinding, sifting, and regrinding grain. Diverse types of mills process the grain differently; some mills are traditional millstones, while modern mills use steel rollers and all produce variation in the end product. The goal of the milling process is gradually extracting the maximum amount of endosperm (the white central part of the grain) while eliminating the bran, which is the roughage on the outside. Each step produces a "stream" of flour (after the sifting process).

The grain undergoing milling can pass through several sets of rollers, each roller descending in thickness as the grain passes through. Each consecutive step in the milling processes removes additional bran from the wheat kernel. The streams or breaks as they are also called are separated individually. The first stages of milling produce the weakest flours in terms of protein content. The final step(s) will produce "clear" flours that are very strong and somewhat darker as they contain pieces of the bran. They are mostly considered useful to strengthen doughs where, for example, the percentage of rye flour is high, and therefore the colour is not so critical, such as wholegrain bread. French flours are created by mixing a blend of different streams of the flour back together to arrive at a predetermined, desired ash content.

Many American mills do not blend individual streams of their flour together but prefer to select blends of flour based on desired dough properties or strength. Consequently, a direct comparison of the flour's ash content does not guarantee equivalency between types. Higher extraction rates in milling generally imply more of the outer endosperm, a darker flour and accordingly high/greater protein content. Additionally, darker or higher extraction flours have a higher ash content. Non-standardised blending taking place in many mills in America which create a scenario whereby a non-standard result in the flour is possible for comparison measures. Then there is a different system in Germany; generally, when comparing to French flours, roughly add a 0 to the French types for the German equivalent. T-55 will become T550 flour (Weekendbakery.com, 2020).

A guide to flour comparison worldwide

I have included two tables on page 23, which will help as a general guide in comparing the complex issue of flour types. They are for use as a guide, they are a rough comparison only, and are not a like for like swap; different milling styles and a different grist or blend of grains give each flour type its diverse character and quality. The first tables' information was from the Dove's Farm website, but I added extra content to include other countries such as Canada and Ireland. Doves Farm offer many great baking resources and make brilliant flour.

Table 1: Flour types comparison table (Doves Farm, 2020)

	Milled from 100% of the whole grain	Extraction rate 85%	White Bread Flour	White Bread Flour	White Flour	Low extraction rate
UK	Wholemeal flour	Brown flour	Strong bread flour	-	Plain flour	Patent flour
Argentina	½	0	00	-	000	0000
Australia	Whole meal flour		Bread flour		Plain flour	Cake/pastry flour
Canada	Whole wheat flour		Bread flour	Bakers patent flour	All-purpose flour	Cake/pastry flour
China	小麦面粉	-	-	-	中筋麵粉	-
Czech Republic	Celozrnná mouka	Hrubá mouka	Polohrubá mouka	-	Hladká mouka	Hladká mouka výběrová 00
France	Farine Intègral 150	110	80	65	55	45
Germany	Vollkorn 1600	1050	812	-	550	405
Holland	Volkorenmeel	Gebuilde bloem	Tarwebloem	-	Patentbloem	Zeeuwse bloem
India	Chakki Atta	Atta	-	-	Maida / Safed	-
Ireland	Wholemeal flour	Brown flour	Strong bakers flour	Bakers flour	Soft flour	Pastry/biscuit flour
Italy	Integrale	Tipo 2	Tipo 1	-	0	00
Poland	Razowa	Sitkowa	Chlebowa	-	Luksusowa	Tortowa
Portugal	Harina Integrale 150	110	80	70	55	45
Slovakia	Celozrnná mouka	Hrubá mouka	Polohrubá mouka	-	Hladká mouka	Hladká mouka výběrová 00
Spain	Harina Integrale 150	110	80	70	55	45
USA	Wholewheat flour	First clear flour	High gluten bread flour	-	All-purpose flour	Pastry flour

Table 2: Flour types, ash and protein content (Weekendbakery.com, 2020)

Ash content	Protien	USA	German	French	Italian	Netherlands	UK
~0.4%	~9%	Pastry flour	405	45	0	Zeeuwse bloem	Pastry flour
~0.55%	~11%	All-purpose flour	550	55	0	Patentbloem	Bakers flour
~0.8%	~14%	High gluten flour	812	80	1	Tarwebloem	Strong bakers
~1%	~15%	First clear flour	1050	110	2	Gebuilde bloem	-
>1.5%	~13%	Whole wheat flour	1700	150	Farina integrale	Volkorenmeel	Wholemeal

Ingredient choices used in great pastry making

Flour for the laminated pastry:

Firstly, the ingredients used should be of the highest possible quality. The flour used for viennoiserie should not be too strong and exhibit good elasticity and when processed into a dough and can be Spelt, T-55, T-65, T-45 or other special flours such as T-45 Gruau Rouge flour. Gruau Rouge is a low extraction very white flour with a lot of elasticity and ideal for viennoiserie. If this cannot be sourced, a baker's bread-making flour combined with a soft pastry type flour in a 75/25% or a 70/30% ratio will give a very favourable result. Tests using 100% Spelt flour have also produced very satisfactory products. The butter, if possible, should also be a special dry, hardened butter with a fat content of between 84-86%.

➢ The type of yeast stated in all the recipes is fresh, compressed yeast

➢ If using dried yeast, use 1/3 of the weights given in the recipes for fresh yeast

➢ Use osmotolerant yeast if available for high sugar/high-fat environment

➢ Lower protein flour with extensible gluten characteristics 11.5 – 12.8% protein

➢ A preferment recipe with 25% of the flour will greatly assist elasticity and handling

➢ Hardened butter with an 84-86% butterfat content with good plasticity qualities

Other ingredients in the pastry

Water

Hydration of the dough is essential, and many bakers use between 46-50% hydration for laminated dough so that the dough consistency matches that of the butter for ease of lamination and superior layering. Use filtered water where possible to remove chlorine and other minerals which may affect fermentation.

Liquid Levain

Adds both extensibility and maturity to the dough, but subtle flavour along with slow leavening, aiding greater volume. Levain assists in the development of an open honeycomb. internal structure.

I use a 1-2-2 liquid levain which is fermented for at least 6 hours before putting it in the dough. That is 1-part starter: 2-parts water: 2 parts-flour.

Yeast

Fresh osmotolerant yeast which is specially used by pastry chefs and bakers for high sugar/high-fat doughs; assisting in more outstanding controlled fermentation. The gassing of the yeast gives stability in the fermentation of the dough. It also adds to the lightness or airiness of the pastry.

Sugar

Sugar acts as a sweetener to the dough but also as a portion of food for the yeast. The sugar also improves the colour of the baking pastry giving it a golden colour.

Salt

Salt gives flavour to the dough; it also has an essential function of both controlling fermentation of the yeast and helps with added colour pigmentation to the pastry. Use organic natural salt where possible. I use organic Oriel sea salt as it is natural salt and free of anti-caking agents and additives.

Malt powder or liquid

Malt is not only good food for yeast development and stability, but it also gives baked pastry a classic chestnut brown colour on the crust. Non-active malt should be used. Honey/glucose are good substitutes if you cannot access malt; it can also be left out of the recipe if required.

Butter used in the dough

Adding butter into the dough gives the pastry a nicer eating quality and the butterfat acts as a lubricant to the gluten in the dough, thereby improving its extensibility in mixing, lamination proofing and baking.

Pâté fermentée

Like liquid levain, Pâté fermentée tends to add a more pronounced flavour to the dough and assists in the elasticity and rolling of the pastry. It also contributes to an open honeycomb structure internally.

Lamination butter used during Coupe Du Monde Chocolatine (CDMC) - Lescure

Beautiful Lescure hardened butter is specially made for excellent flavour and quality laminated viennoiserie production. The higher fat content/lower moisture content enables the dough to form beautiful layers easier, and the butter also has a higher melting point which helps keep the delicious flaky layers intact together throughout the process of production.

Chocolate sticks Valrhona used during CDMC

The chocolate sticks were provided for the Chocolatine World Cup by the globally famous Valrhona chocolate brand. Of a premium quality, Valrhona chocolate bars are specially made for baking and do not burn in the oven.

Egg wash

Egg wash is the varnish on the pastry, not only does it give a beautiful shine and colour, but it also adds flavour, and it helps the layers at the top of the chocolatine to stick together and not fly off the top when baking. See recipe page 74.

Understanding the butter

Butter is an emulsion of oil and water made from dairy cream. Butter comes in many forms including salted, unsalted, country butter, clarified butter, ghee, spreadable butter, fractionated butter, recombined butter and dry butter to name but a few. The texture achieved by butter is as a result of the degree of processing given the butter during the manufacturing process. Like chocolate, the fat in butter undergoes a tempering factor which establishes a crystalline network which results in the establishment of the smooth texture which butter exhibits as raw material and a portion of food. Salt is added for both flavour and to extend the shelf life of the butter. Butter has many applications and functions in laminated pastry making. In the croissant dough, which is made before lamination, regular soft butter is added as an enriching agent, and it also contributes towards a shortening effect in the finished product, by lubricating the gluten formed in the mixed dough. I do not recommend using home-made butter for lamination as it is too soft, has too much water and too little butterfat. A harder butter is therefore, used for the lamination process. This hard butter is made from fermented cream and has had some of the liquid components removed to add more hard fat. Plasticity and melting point are the properties bakers seek in this type of butter. If the butter is too hard and lacking in plasticity, the butter will fracture in the lamination process leading to uneven distribution and layer formation.

Butter is typically made up of the following components:

- Butterfat   80.0 – 83.0 %
- Water   15.6 – 17.6 %

Proteins and fat-soluble vitamins and minerals 1-1.2 % include:

- Phosphorus
- Calcium
- Vitamins A, D and E
- Available as salted or unsalted butter

(Ranken, et al., 1997).

Butterfat crystals are classified as existing in the following states

- Alpha (α)
- Beta prime (β!)
- Beta (β)

The alpha (α) form are the least stable of the butter crystals and have the lowest melting point and generally scattered randomly in the butter. The beta prime (β!) or intermediate stage tend to align themselves at right angles in alternating rows and are larger than the alpha crystalline form. They are more stable and have a higher melting point than the alpha crystals. In this form, they form a smooth surface which is ideal for lamination as the smooth crystalline surfaces allow the butter layers to glide and create even layers displaying the best plasticity. The beta (β) crystals are the largest crystalline form in butter and tend to form in parallel rows.

These crystals are the most stable of the three states and have the highest melting point (Brown, 2018). The shape and type of butter crystal govern their practicality in both pastry making and food preparation. A common characteristic of butterfat is that the melting point of the butter increases as the crystal size increases. The first form, the alpha (α) crystal the smallest state, the middle-sized beta prime (β!) or intermediate stage, to the final largest stage, the beta (β) crystal (Brown, 2018).

The tempering of butter for croissant sheets takes place at the manufacturing stage of the process, and the plasticity and consistency of the butter are determined by both the correct tempering and the accurate addition of hard fat balanced by the removal of oils and liquid components. Tempering rigid butter sheets by passing it through a pastry sheeter or hydraulic press raises the temperature of the fat slightly leading to the alignment and formation of the beta prime crystals in the butterfat, which gives good plasticity during processing and texture to the finished product. The rheological answer of roll-in butter arises from a colloidal grid of different types of fat crystals. The network or matrix formed by the fat's manufacturing process and crystallisation influences its lamination characteristics.

To ensure that good lamination characteristics are maintained throughout the process of making croissants, the crystallisation must be judiciously performed by controlling the temperature of the butter at all times (Rodriguez & Merangioni, 2018). Lamination butter is normally plasticised as it is prepared for incorporation in pastry by a process known in French as Beurrage. The butter is placed between a plastic sheet or parchment paper and beaten down with a rolling pin to give plasticity to the butter and also to encourage the formation of small crystals to the butter's crystal network. The most favourable temperature range for working with hard (dry) croissant butter is between 7-11°C, whereas standard types of butter with lower fat content are most plastic between 16-21°C (Stamm, 2011). I find the best working temperature with 84% butterfat at about 9°C.

Temperature control – desired dough temperature calculation

Bakers and pastry chefs make bread and pastry all over the world, from tropical areas to colder Northern and Southern Hemispheres. This means the working temperatures we all have in daily work is different, some are hot, some are cold. Because of these other geographic locations, the temperature in a bakery or home kitchen will vary greatly. In a bakery for instance, if the temperature is 10°C overnight, it follows, that all ingredients in the bakery, such as flour, sugar and the equipment are also at the same temperature of 10°C. Generally, croissant dough is made to arrive at a mixed temperature of 24-26°C. To manage the temperature so that consistent pastry can be made, it is crucial to have control over the final temperature of the dough.

There is a formula, a good rule of thumb to roughly calculate the dough temp or DT so that when the dough is finished mixing it is at the desired or optimum temperature to promote fermentation. This is called the Desired Dough Temperature or DDT. Yeast types used in these doughs may be fresh, dry or active dried yeasts. It is essential to read the instructions on using different types of yeast as some require hydration before use, fresh yeast can be mixed directly into the dough as instant yeast. If using active dry yeast, for example, this yeast needs to be hydrated/have water added to it to kick off the fermentation. Converting from the use of fresh yeast to dry yeast in a recipe is generally 1/3rd dry to fresh yeast weight. So, for example, if a recipe calls for 30g of fresh yeast in a recipe, to compensate for the conversion to dry yeast, only 10g should be used. We all know that yeast likes both food and warmth to thrive, and this is why all recipes should have what is called the Desired Dough Temperature or DDT.

In the case of croissant dough when mixed, the DDT should be between 24-26°C to kick start the gassing process. The flour you store and use in your mix will be at the temperature the room you are working in is. Allowing the baker to control the finished temperature of the dough is essential for consistent quality and a simple formula will guide you to achieving your DDT. If you work in sweltering temperatures, tropical climate for example without air conditioning, you may need to chill your flour, water and other ingredients in a fridge overnight before use. Generally, using flour at your room temperature or FT requires that you to calculate the temperature of the water WT to arrive at a correct DDT. Committing to memory this information should be a daily part of a bakers' decision-making process. Simply described, the rule of thumb is *"Twice the required dough temperature minus the flour temperature gives you the water temperature required".* The formula to calculate the Desired Dough Temperature is as follows:

Desired Dough Temperature x 2-Flour Temperature = Water Temperature to use in the dough

$$\textbf{DDTx2 – FT = WT}$$

From our recipes, you will see that 26°C is DDT. For this example, we will take the temperature of 22°C as the FT. From these two figures, we can calculate the correct water temperature required to arrive at the Desired Dough Temperature.

Example 1 Warm climate:

We want to make a dough 26°C, and it is 22°C in the bakery.

26°C x 2 = 52°C - 22°C (your room temperature) = 30°C, the water temperature you need to add to create a dough @26°C if your room temperature is 22°C.

Example 2 Cold climate:

We want to make a dough 26°C, and it is 10°C in the bakery.

26°C x 2 = 52°C - 10°C (your room temperature) = 42°C, the water temperature you need to create a dough @26°C if your room temperature is 10°C.

These examples demonstrate the need to control the dough temperature by adjusting the water temperature. The formula generally considers the friction factor/the heat generated and temperature rise by a mixer when mixing dough.

Understanding the dough

Dough rheology is a science, and it is not my intention to get into the science of it in this book. Laminated dough generally has a lower hydration level to bread or brioche dough. A good rule of thumb is to use 500g of total liquid (water/milk/egg combined) per 1000g flour or a 50% hydration. If the dough is too soft (over hydrated) it will be challenging to combine the dough and butter as the dough will stretch/flow over the butter like the crest of a wave, giving a large lump of dough at the ends and the sides of the pastry block. If the dough is too tight, cracking and difficulty in processing will occur. If the dough is too warm, when the butter is placed on it, the butter will begin to soften/melt into oil, leading to poor lamination. Additionally, if the dough is too cold, it will fracture when passed through a pastry sheeter as the dough will snap.

If the butter is too cold, the butter will also crack, and improper layers will form. The dough and butter should have a similar consistency and temperature, which will aid the formation of desired even layers throughout the pastry. The ideal temperature range for commencing lamination of the dough is between 1.1°C-3.3°C. The dough is generally made the previous day and given a short mixing time. The dough should be cold fermented overnight to allow the full development of the dough and the relaxation of the gluten formed in the mixing process. The cold fermentation also develops the structure and aromatic qualities of the dough, which help give the croissant pastry its distinctive taste and texture. The dough should be degassed by hand or through a reversible sheeter and placed in the freezer for a few minutes to ensure that it is at the optimum temperature for further processing. Additionally, this stretching of the dough in the sheeter not only further degasses the dough but it also importantly causes protein alignment of the gluten in one direction. It is important to remember to rotate the pastry 90° at each stage of the lamination, i.e., the lock-in, the first fold and any subsequent folds. In this way, the pastry is stretched equally in different directions, which will help eliminate shrinkage following final sheeting. Care in the process ensures that the laminated structure of the dough/butter layers remains intact throughout the process. In summary, the pastry temperature should be controlled at all stages to arrest all fermentation during the lamination, sheeting and cutting stages until the pastry is placed into the proofer to activate the yeast for the final fermentation phase.

Maintaining a sourdough starter

In some of the recipes in this book, I use my sourdough starter "Covid Culture-2020" to add elasticity, acidity and depth of flavour to the dough. If you are already a sourdough baker, you will already be familiar with the process, but if not, I will describe the process briefly below. As this book is about laminated pastry, I won't be deviating off the topic much, but I will be providing step by step guidance and detail on how to maintain your existing starter and when to use it for making the dough for your pastry.

Recipe for starter refresh

Ingredients	Quantity	Ratio
Strong flour	50g	2
Water (40-42°C)	50g	2
Liquid starter culture	25g	1
	Total 125g	

Process of preparation

1. Using a clean bowl, whisk the starter and the warm water together, add the flour and mix well to wet all the flour. Place in a clean glass jar with a lid loosely fitted.
2. Allow the starter to ferment at a warm room temperature of 26-28°C for about 6 hours before use. Pour it into the dough making water, it should float. Whisk them together with the yeast in the recipe, then make your dough.
3. Allow the remaining starter to complete fermentation and transfer the liquid sourdough to the fridge @4°C after 18 hours.

Important liquid sourdough makeup points

By adding the warm water to the starter, the liquid and warmth of the water will stimulate the starter to activate. Adding the flour provides the food source for the starter to feed and grow. I always use a glass jar for hygiene reasons when growing starters, and I mark the level of the starter with an elastic band. It provides a good visual indicator to watch the performance of the liquid sourdough as it grows. An active sourdough should at least double if not triple in size. If you think of your starter as a pet or farm animal and tend to it in this manner of thought; it needs water, food, attention and warmth to thrive. Additionally, like any relationship, it requires consistency to keep it fresh, healthy and prevent it from going sour 😊.

Storage of liquid sourdough

Sourdough should be kept in a sealed jar in the fridge @3-4°C. It can be stored for several days in this state and then refreshed again later as described earlier. The stored liquid sourdough can also be used as an ingredient in the pastry.

The need to rotate pastry through 90° on every fold

When making all types of laminated pastry, it is essential to rotate the pastry block at a 90° angle on each rolling stage throughout the process after folding. The science behind this is that the gluten matrix aligns in a two-dimensional phase and form long elastic chains when stretched in one direction. If you can imagine, as a child, having an elastic band in your hand and you stretch it, then release the tension, the elastic band returns to the shape it has been formed into. However, if you keep stretching it, harder and harder; eventually, the elastic band will snap and sheeter. The return of the elastic band to its original shape is known as elastic recoil, and this can be seen when making pastry as a shrinking of the sheeted pastry when folding or cutting. The elastic limit of a rubber band is the limit at which, if stretched beyond this point, it will snap and lose its original form and snap. Dough reacts similarly during lamination, and by rotating the pastry through 90° each time you are sheeting the pastry, you stretch and realign the gluten matrix in the dough at a right angle to the previous sheeting stage of the pastry making. Resting is also most important as it allows the pastry block time to recover its elasticity from the rolling and sheeting phase. Following the lock-in, the pastry is sheeted and folded. The black arrows below in Figure 1. Indicate the direction that the gluten matrix in the pastry has been stretched. In order to balance the elasticity and create an elastic equilibrium throughout the pastry; preventing shrinkage is vital and the pastry needs to be stretched equally in all directions; hence the need to rotate the pastry 90°during each sheeting cycle. The arrows in Figure 1 indicate the stretching and the resistance of the gluten matrix, or elastic recoil acting in the pastry as it is processed. As the gluten matrix stretches, so too does it develop resistance and pulls back, much like stretching an elastic band and releasing it. In this way, an elastic equilibrium is established within the pastry, and the pastry is in balance, shrinking is neutralised by even forces acting within the pastry by this gluten matrix.

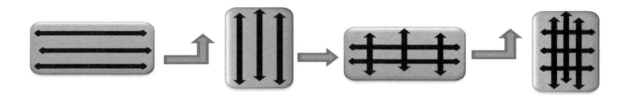

Figure 1: Gluten matrix visual during the sheeting process

Proofing pastry in the home

While the makeup, recipe and shaping of yeasted laminated pastry are deemed by most as the hardest part of making this style of pastry, all the hard work invested in making it can be lost by incorrect proofing. The proofing process can be a deal-breaker as to whether you end up with a perfect honeycomb structure or not. Many home bakers do not have the luxury of temperature and humidity-controlled proofers to use as a tool in producing exceptional pastry. There is the Brød & Taylor home proofer/yoghurt maker; I have posted a link on it in the section of other online resources at the end of the book. It is expensive but has great ratings from those who have purchased it, and it can be used to make yoghurt, hold melted chocolate; and folds away to the size of a large book for storage when finished using it. If you cannot buy one, or it is not in the budget don't worry, proofing can be achieved in a variety of ways. If you live in a warm/humid climate, for example, or work in a warm home or kitchen, simply covering the pastries in a plastic bag to prevent skinning will work just fine. You can prevent the proofing pastry from sticking to the plastic by standing inverted tall glasses spaced out on your baking trays. The pastry can also be placed (again covered) in a hot press or airing cupboard. Proofing can also be achieved using a domestic oven with a few careful procedures, and I will outline a sample procedure below. The thing to understand about proofing is that there are two very important elements at play in the proofing process:

1. Heat (to stimulate fermentation or gassing in the dough)
2. Humidity (to prevent skinning of the dough and allow maximum expansion in proof)

The heat stimulates the yeast, but cannot be too warm; otherwise, the yeast will perish, and the butter layers will melt. Humidity prevents the expanding pastry from skinning on the surface, and therefore expansion of the pastries can take place. If there is no humidity, a thick skin will form on the outer surfaces, and the pastry will not be able to proof/expand properly due to this hard skin surrounding it. Most domestic ovens have a light, check and see what temperature your oven generates with just the light left on after one hour.

If it gets too hot after one hour (over 28°C) reduce the time. Additionally, many ovens have a defrost cycle which can be pre-programmed to very low temperatures of -20°C to -30°C. If these pre-sets exist on your domestic oven, humidity can be introduced by pouring boiling water into a small tray placed at the bottom of the oven. Be sure to place your tray of pastries in the middle deck of the oven, pour the boiling water into the bottom tray and close the oven door.

Figure 2: Deep tray wrapped in cling film

Another simple way of proofing where you have adequate heat, but no humidity, is to proof the pastries in a deep tin. Simply place the pastries into the deep pan shape, egg wash and wrap the baking tin tightly in clingfilm. Finally, no matter which technique you use to proof the pastry, it may take some hours and patience is essential. Do not bake the pastry until you can see the layers separating and the pastry jiggles like wobbly jelly when shaken gently; jiggle videos are in the resources section at the end of the book.

Baking using different oven types

During baking, the heat source and balance of that heat in the oven is critical to getting a good bake on pastry. As the pastry heats up in the oven, the water in the dough and in the butter layers vaporize from water into steam with the heat of the oven. As the steam trapped in the layers expands, the dough inflates, and the layers created separate from each other, giving volume to the pastry. Lipids in the butter basically fry the pastry, resulting in the light, airy, flaky qualities associated with puff paste and viennoiserie. Bakers bake in different ovens all over the world. Some are domestic ovens for home baking, some are commercial ovens built robustly for heavy-duty work.In my experiences of baking in various countries, bakeries and schools, for over three decades, all the ovens I have used have their own unique quirkiness. To clarify my statement, generally, ovens are made mainly of metal, insulation, glass, stone, and various electric or gas components to generate heat for baking. They have doors made of thermal glass, metal or a combination of both which allow the baker to load/unload and see into the baking chamber while baking. All ovens are screwed or welded together, metal on metal; and over time, due to this expansion/contraction, the insulation and thermal efficiency of the oven can deteriorate. I am not covering brick or wood-fired ovens as they are generally not used for baking viennoiserie. All ovens are by their nature subjected to the extremes of heating and cooling daily. As ovens age, all this heating and cooling can cause the oven to be less efficient than a new oven as the metal in the ovens/door seals, the screws and welds holding it together and heating elements suffer wear and tear with continued use.

Insulation can also deteriorate, causing further heat differentials. Thermostats can again fail or give the baker erroneous readings of the actual oven temperature. A small stand-alone oven thermometer can be purchased in most kitchenware shops and can be used to verify an ovens existing thermometers integrity. Ovens can develop hot and cold spots, and a baker using an oven daily gets to know his oven very well. He can see that perhaps the back left of the oven is cooler than the front left and knows to rotate the trays in this part of the oven halfway through the bake to get an even colour on his batch of baked goods. An infrared (IR) thermometer is an excellent and useful tool for measuring oven temperature. The temperatures for baking given in the book reflect the oven temperatures I have baked with and my experience in using commercial ovens daily.

Most small viennoiserie pieces bake in deck ovens at 200°C for roughly 20 minutes and in convection ovens at 175°C for 16-18 minutes. Commercial electric multi-deck ovens also have separate controls for the heating elements of the top, bottom and door of each deck in the oven. The controls range from a figure of 1 to 10 in baking intensity, with 1 being the lowest or gentlest heat setting and 10 being the most intense heat. The settings for baking viennoiserie on these type of deck ovens are generally Top heat 7, Bottom heat 1 to 2, and door heat 6 to 7, but please bear in mind that all ovens are different and heat/bake differently.

Every oven will lose temperature when you open the door, especially convection ovens, that said, they also recover quicker than deck ovens and are the professionals' choice of oven for baking viennoiserie. Viennoiserie generally has almost 1/3rd more volume when baked in a convection oven than the same product baked in a deck oven. This is due to the rapid recovery to temperature of convection ovens, and the fan accelerated air within, which can penetrate the pastry quickly, heats the core rapidly and as a result bake time is reduced. Deck ovens are mainly used in baking bread and confectionery. They are not as good at baking viennoiserie as a fan oven, as the heat method is known as a dead heat bake, i.e. heat conducted by the oven sole and roof via electrical elements on the top and the chamber itself.

There is commonly no fan in a deck oven, but some superior and expensive models have fans for each deck too. Deck ovens are better at retaining heat than convection ovens, but they can take a very long time to recover the heat lost during loading the oven if it is too low. I have witnessed an oven at 220°C, fully loaded with bread drop to 150°C and taking 30 minutes before reaching 220°C. Temperature and time considerations need to be made, whether you fully load an oven or are only baking one tray in the oven as the partially filled oven will bake one tray faster than say three and lose less heat in loading. As the oven door is open a shorter time, and the weight of one tray and product will heat faster than three times that. For example, when you put a tray of pastry into an oven; the weight of the metal tray plus the weight of the pastries you are baking will rob the oven of some of its heat. The oven will lose between 20°C to 50°C, depending on the oven type and whether the oven is filled to capacity, or only has one tray in it after loading. All these factors will determine the oven recovery time, which will be unique to your particular oven. The pastries will be baked at a much lower heat as the oven struggles to rise in temperature; the thermostat will be calling for heat all the time. The net result is a longer bake time, inferior product, and a drier product, as baking at a lower temperature longer will dry out the product. A working example of the above is when I fill my convection oven with croissants.

1. There are 6 trays@ 800g each - 4800g of metal

2. 60 pastries @70g 4200g - of pastry

That's 9000g of room temperature materials that require heating up to my bake temperature of 170°C, it's like chucking ice into a drink, it cools it down rapidly. It takes a lot of time to transfer enough energy into the tins and product to get back to the correct baking temperature. For example, I set the convection oven @220°C, load it, close the oven door and reset the thermostat to 170°C to bake my product. If I did not do this, the oven would fall to 120°C and the products would not be very nice due to longer bake time, drying out and would lose that boldness in the bake, that a sharp, hot oven gives to products. The oven I use drops over 50°C after loading, so I always factor for this when baking. Becoming familiar with your own oven is easy by simply measuring the drop of the oven temperature when loaded fully, and an Infrared thermometer (IR thermometer) is an excellent tool for establishing this.

The Bakers' % explained

Many people simply have a blockage when it comes to numbers. I have many people request online to explain the bakers% or Bakers Maths as it is also known. If you can count to 10, you can do it! If you can count to 100, it will be the easiest thing you ever did. Bakers maths or Bakers % simply mean that the main ingredient, flour in all their forms in a recipe, such as wholemeal, white, rye etc.is always 100%. All other ingredients are measured against the quantity of flour the recipe. While weight quantities can go up or down according to mix or batch sizes, the percentages will always remain constant. If you have a great recipe, it can be scaled up to commercial quantities or down for home baking without the recipe altering in any way as the percentages maintain the exact ratios of ingredients during the conversion. The hydration of dough is the percentage of total liquids in a recipe in relation to total flour weight. The usual liquids used in pastry making include water, egg and milk. I have included both water and egg in this exercise to demonstrate hydration levels in a dough. Below, I set out an example of recipe conversion with bakers' percentage, which can be applied to all recipes:

Sample Bread Recipe expressed in Bakers %

Ingredient	Weight in g small recipe	Bakers %	Weight in g large recipe
Bread flour	80	80%	8,000
Wholemeal	20	20%	2,000
Flour total:	**100**	**100%**	**10,000**
Water	68	68%	6,800
Egg	5	5%	500
Hydration total:	**73**	**73%**	**7,300**
Salt	2	2%	200
Butter	4	4%	400
Fresh yeast	2	2%	200

To break down the main components in the recipe, I have separately analysed two types of flour and two types of liquid to accurately measure the hydration of the dough. The above example uses 100g of flour in the recipe, 80% white flour and 20% wholemeal and is expressed as a combined total being 100%. Water 68% and egg 5% combine to give a collective hydration figure of 73%. All other ingredients are similarly expressed, salt 2%, butter 4% and fresh yeast 2%. By examining the bakers % at first glance, the baker can ascertain whether the dough is highly hydrated (over 70%) or in the case of croissant dough, a stiff dough of 50% hydration. Depending on flour types used in a pastry recipe, I have successfully made croissant with varying hydration levels and recommend a hydration level of between 46% -57% depending on flour strength and flours' adsorption ability (damaged starch in the milling process increases its adsorption abilities). Below in Figure 3, is a viennoiserie recipe for croissant pastry I have used many times. I created an expanded recipe spreadsheet which includes all ingredients in the recipe, the weight in grams and the bakers % of each ingredient. Additionally, I include the batch yield, the total % butter in the pastry, which includes the sum of the butter in the dough plus lamination butter combined. Finally,

I have colour coded the spreadsheet below; flour is gold, liquids are blue, and butter is of course yellow. Hydration is 50% in this sample recipe.

Base Croissant Recipe

Ingredients	1 Mix	1/2 Mix	Based on flour 100%	
			Bakers %	**Hydration %**
	Kg / g	Kg / g	500	50.00
Overnight dough Stage 1				
Strong Flour	500	250	100.0 %	
Egg	50	25	10.0 %	
Water	200	100	40.0 %	
Sugar	45	23	9.0 %	
Fresh yeast	35	18	7.0 %	
Milk powder	25	13	5.0 %	
Salt	7	4	1.4 %	
Butter	25	13	5.0 %	
Dough head weight	887	444	**Butter on Dough %**	Total Butter % in both Dough & Lamination
Lamination dough Stage 2				
Laminating butter	225	113	25.4	30.4
Total Batch weight	1,112	556		
Yield	15	7		
Scaling wt in grams	75			

Figure 3: Working example of bakers% use in a recipe sheet

Core temperature and chilling pastry using ice blankets

A crucial part of good pastry making is to control both the fermentation of the dough and the temperature of the butter together at all stages throughout the makeup process. It is most essential to prevent the pastry skinning or proofing throughout the lamination stage as uneven layers will form in the pastry. By using various means of cooling the pastry, fermentation is delayed; both the dough and the butter remain cool throughout the process. Industrial fridges, freezers, blast chillers and Cryopack® ice blankets are essential tools for pastry production. In many professional kitchens and bakeries, they have an airconditioned room to control the environmental temperature for pastry consistency. Most home bakers do not have the luxury of such space or equipment. It is common practice even in many culinary schools lacking equipment such as blast chillers, to simply wrap the pastry in a plastic sheet and chill it down on a metal tray in the freezer. It is essential to wrap the pastry in a thick plastic sheet to prevent frostbite on the surface. Additionally, when using the ice blankets, the plastic keeps the pastry from becoming wet and sticky. When the pastry is chilled in this way, the bottom part of the pastry in contact with the frozen tray will begin to cool rapidly through touching or conduction. The sides and top of the pastry take longer to chill as they are relying on the circulation of chilled air or convection to cool them and this creates an imbalance in the chilling process. Often, the bottom, corners and edges of the pastry begin to freeze quicker than the rest of the pastry and cause problems when processing, as the freezing is not even throughout the block of pastry and in different areas, the pastry has different temperatures.

It is critical that the pastry is chilled quickly and not frozen during the makeup process, as freezing damages water crystals both in the dough and the water and fat crystals in the butter. If frozen, the dough portion of the pastry will split and crack, and the butter element will become hard, brittle and shatter into pieces, giving a marbled aspect to the pastry and destroying the layers created in the makeup process. Pastry makers in the past have often used two frozen metal trays to chill pastry down quickly. The trays, placed like a sandwich on the sheeted pastry top and bottom, cool the outside layers of the pastry quickly. However, the pastry rapidly takes all the coldness out of the trays, and they need to be chilled several times again to be effective at maintaining a low temperature.

A modern approach is to use "Cryopack® Ice Blankets". These are available on Amazon and are worth the investment to serious pastry makers. For home bakers or hobbyists, two packs of frozen corn or peas work equally well as ice blankets, for small quantities of pastry which is an inexpensive option and yields excellent results https://youtu.be/-WZ9w0gPjyg . I first saw the use of ice blankets (see Figure 4), in pastry processing at the Coupe du Monde de la Boulangerie competitions, Paris, in the mid-2000s by team USA's viennoiserie candidate Peter Yuen and some of the Asian viennoiserie candidates. Ice blankets are excellent for rapidly chilling down laminated pastry as the pastry block is encapsulated top and bottom, physically touching the ice blanket. As a result of this direct contact between pastry and the ice blanket, a very efficient, uniform and rapid chilling of the pastry dough block is possible.

Figure 4: Ice blankets in use covering pastry block

In the illustration in Figure 5 page 44, a folded block of pastry (gold) is illustrated with a book fold or a 4, and it is wrapped in an ice blanket (blue). The pastry is touching the ice blanket surface, and it is this direct contact that chills the pastry down quickly. The thicker the pastry, the longer it takes to chill to the core. On the left side of the diagram, the pastry block is much thicker (30mm) than the one on the right (15mm). The thick black line illustrates the core or centre of the pastry block. The pastry chills from the outside into the core; when wrapped in ice blankets, pastry has the dual effect of cooling by the ice blankets top and bottom.

The thickness of the pastry, when inserted into the ice blanket, is important, as the thinner it is, the more rapidly the pastry will chill down. In the diagram on the left, the ice blanket needs to chill through 15mm of pastry top and bottom, and there is a danger that the pastry will begin to move/proof in the core before it can be influenced by the chilling of the ice blanket. On the right side of the illustration, the same pastry block is sheeted down to 15mm. The ice blanket must only chill through 7.5mm of pastry to get to the core, and as a result, it cools twice as quickly. Therefore, I always recommend sheeting folded pastry to between 12-15mm before chilling in ice blankets.

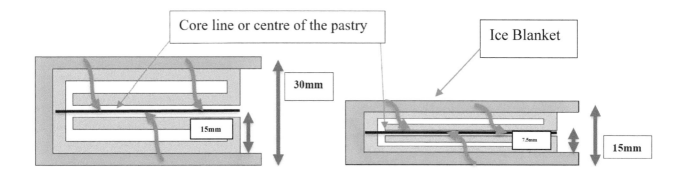

Figure 5: Importance of pinning out the pastry prior to chilling

Understanding core temperature in proofing pastry

As discussed in understanding the core temperature in chilling pastry earlier, the centre of something is generally referred to as the core or the middle. When shaping pastry, especially Croissant, Pain Chocolat, Pain aux Raisin or any pastry that is rolled up when shaping, it will have a spiral profile with layers coiled on top of each other, a core or central point and an outside. The pastry is a poor conductor of heat, and this is especially true when proofing coiled pastries such as croissant and pain au chocolat. The outside of the pastry in a proofer will slowly begin to heat up, but it will take some time for the heat to permeate throughout the pastry to the core. Generally, croissant pastry is proofed at approximately 26°C-27°C for two to three hours. It is not possible to proof croissant pastry at a higher temperature, as the butter will melt inside the layers and fold to oil, destroying the layers that have been created during lamination. As illustrated in Figure 6, page 44, the outside surface begins to heat up and proof.

It takes time for the proofer heat to get to the core of the pastry and heat it up. The temperature of the proofer slowly transfers from surrounding air to the surface and then through the proofing pastry to the core. Honeycomb crumb structure is a good indicator of a successfully proofed pastry. A thick and gummy, non-aerated core is an indicator of insufficient proof time and baking the pastry before the pastry core has opened out and proofed fully. It is possibly the most common fault in baking laminated yeasted pastry.

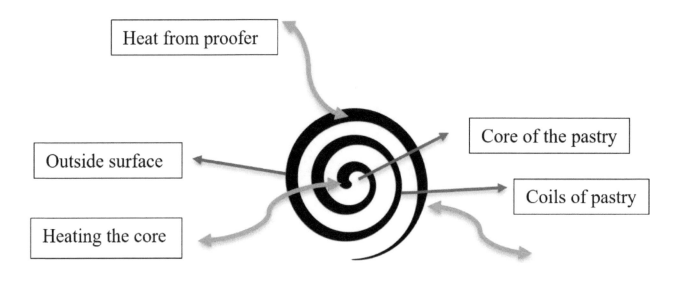

Figure 6: Coiled pastry proofing illustration

Recipes used in this publication

I have relied on many different recipes in this book, all of them work very well and have slight variances between them. I do not have one favourite recipe as they all serve the purpose of furthering my existing studies and understanding of pastry making. Additionally, professional bakers and home bakers alike will have their own favourite recipes and secret ingredients. Still, they can apply many of the techniques used in the book to improve the outcomes of their own products and procedures. Knowledge, practice and consistency are key elements in perfecting laminated pastry making. Hydration of 48-52% of the dough will give a dough that is easy to handle and will hold its form and shape easily. My own personal target hydration is approximately 50% for mostly all of the laminated pastry that I make, but this may require adjustment depending on the country, the flour available and the strength of that flour. If you increase hydration beyond this, the dough is sticky and requires a lot of dusting flour. It does not keep its shape well and will flow in proof spreading out on the tray as it bakes and generally not as bold as lower hydrated pastry. The visibility of layers is also affected by increased hydration; something to consider!

Processing factors

- A poolish preferment may be used in the main dough up to a maximum of 10% dough weight if your flour is very strong as it adds elasticity and flavour to the dough
- Pate fermentée can also be added to the dough and also adds flavour and elasticity
- Dough mixing times mentioned are using a standard Hobart type mixer with a dough hook: 4 minutes on first speed, 4 - 5 minutes on second speed. Times will vary depending on the machine type
- After mixing the dough is covered with plastic and given a 45 minutes bulk fermentation at room temperature. Sheet out the dough to between 12-15 mm. Wrap the dough in plastic and place in the fridge overnight at a temperature of between 3-4°C for 12-16 hrs
- A cold fermentation process gives the best flavour, and both relaxes and strengthens the dough, imparting good elasticity for processing and lamination
- Dough hydration should be a figure of between 48% to 51% depending on the type of flour used
- Ideally, the dough and butter should have roughly the same consistency when sheeting
- In the morning, upon taking the fermented dough from the fridge, DO NOT KNEAD/MANIPULATE THE DOUGH! Otherwise, you will toughen the dough, and it will shrink from elastic recoil
- Simply flatten it down with a rolling pin and sheet out the dough to 10mm, wrap in plastic and place in freezer 10 minutes
- The dough should be chilled to as close to 3°C before locking in the butter
- Butter should ideally be shaped into one thin rectangular block the day before and stored in a refrigerator. Before use, take the butter out of the fridge and leave aside for a few minutes to soften slightly. It should be malleable like putty and not hard
- **A YouTube video tutorial on how to make the butter block on a pastry sheeter is attached in the link below**

➢ The butter is ready for lamination when of plastic consistency roughly at a temperature of 7-11°C. Prod the butter with a finger, and if the finger makes an indentation without melting the butter, it is ready for use (see it in the video).

➢ The butter and dough in the pastry increase in temperature due to outside atmospheric temperature, and also from the friction of rolling the dough. On mechanical sheeters, the temperature of the pastry can increase by as much as 1°C per pass from friction alone.

How to prepare a butter block on YouTube by Jimmy Griffin:

Figure 7: One-minute croissant butter block technique (Griffin, 2015)

Follow the link to see 1 kg butter block made on a pastry sheeter: https://youtu.be/Cj0gEXtXexw

Lock-in and lamination numbering system

There is much confusion over the names, the types of folds used, and the number of folds used in pastry making. The universal numbering system is a more accurate and appropriate method of describing and defining how the pastry is folded after the butter is added to the dough. Numbers are international and provide a global understanding of lamination sequences. The first stage is always known as the lock-in phase. The lock-in number will always appear as a bold number at the beginning of a sequence, for example, like a **3** or a **5** in this book to instil the learning objective of the universal numbering system. There are two composite ingredient components in laminated pastry making systems:

1. A dough component
2. A fat/butter component

The two components mentioned above are the same for puff pastry production, the only difference is that in the case of croissant dough, the dough is yeasted. For lamination to take place, the butter/fat must be encapsulated into the lock-in is referred to as the first number in the sequence of pastry making, which as mentioned above will be highlighted and identified in bold text throughout this document. The first number in the pastry laminating system is always the lock-in number where you "lock-in" the butter block between the dough.

Dough touching points

If you take a piece of dough in your fingers, stretch it, fold it over on itself and compress/squeeze it, it does not form two separate layers of dough. As children, many of us have experienced this phenomenon while chewing, stretching gum in our mouths and fingers. With the dough, the force of compression on the dough and the stickiness of the dough cause the two outside dough layers to bond and become one layer. Applying this principle to croissant pastry making as the dough encapsulates the butter and is rolled out to create a thin sheet of pastry; the dough always remains on the outside of the pastry. The butter is always remaining in between the formed dough layers. When the sheeted dough is folded into a book form 4 or a half fold 3, the outside dough layers stack on top of each other and these two layers or pleats of dough I refer to as a "Dough Touching Point" or DTP for short (see Figure 8).

When compressed by rolling, the two dough contact points become one layer of dough. As a result, you must factor this disappearance of one layer when calculating total layers in the pastry during each folding process. The formula is very simple and straightforward, you subtract one layer from the total number of layers for each dough touching point. Given that the most common forms of folding are a 4-fold or a 3-fold, the maths become easy. Applying this principle to any number of folds, the following numbers apply for exact layer calculation.

- A 6-fold has five Dough Touching Points   minus 5 layers
- A 5-fold has four Dough Touching Points   minus 4 layers
- A 4-fold has three Dough Touching Points   minus 3 layers
- A 3-fold has two Dough Touching Points   minus 2 layers
- A 2-fold has one Dough Touching Point   minus 1 layer

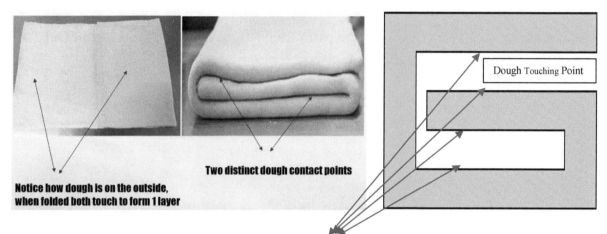

Figure 8: Explaining dough touching points in a 3-fold

Steps and stages of preparing fermented laminated pastry

3-4-3 system process overview

The 3-4-3 system is possibly the most popular and widespread used sequence of lamination in the world. It is used for croissant, pain aux raisins, and chocolatines, as well as many other types of pastry. When completed, the pastry will have 25 layers alternating layers. It produces a lovely leafy exterior and a honeycombed interior. While there are many stages and ingredient choices used in making laminated pastry, overleaf is a bulleted introduction and overview of the procedures/sequence/sequences used to turn raw materials of dough and butter into a finished block of pastry. I will cover different recipes and several different lamination systems in later chapters of the book, such as:

1. **3**-4-3 (**3**-3-4) (**5**-6)   25 layers (all have the same quantity of layers)
2. **3**-4-4   33 layers
3. **3**-3-3-3   55 layers
4. **5**-4-3   49 layers

Additionally, I will cover twin lamination, cross lamination, multi-colour lamination and bicolor pastries. These specific lamination systems will be explained in greater detail. Classic croissant making typically employs the **3**-4-3 system. Still, generally, once the first stage - the lock in is complete, the pastry is sheeted (rolled out into a thin sheet) and folded into pleats of pastry into a rectangular block; the purpose of which is to build up a structure of alternating dough/butter/dough layers. These alternating layers give the pastry its structure and impart flakiness and lightness when combined with controlled fermentation. It is most important to always completely wrap the pastry in plastic to prevent skinning of the outer dough surface throughout the process, and I have included a YouTube video on how to do this properly. The basic steps employed for a **3**-4-3 system are as follows:

➢ Mixing of the dough and preparation of the butter block while the dough mixes

➢ Overnight fermentation of the dough in a fridge 3-4°C

➢ Pinning out the dough to a rectangle and placing the butter block on the dough

➢ Sealing the butter block between 2 layers of dough (**3** lock-in) like a sandwich

➢ Locking in the butter between the dough to create alternate dough/butter layers

➢ Sheeting out the lock-in to a thickness of approximately 3.5- 4 mm

➢ The 1st fold of the pastry using a 4-fold (book fold)

➢ Resting of the pastry in the freezer

➢ Sheeting out the pastry with its first fold to a thickness of approximately 6mm

➢ The 2nd fold or folding of the pastry using a 3-fold (half turn)

➢ Pinning the pastry out to 12mm and covering in plastic

➢ Resting of the pastry block in the freezer

➢ Sheeting out the pastry in preparation for cutting; cutting and shaping of the pastry

➢ Proofing of the pastry; egg washing the pastry, baking and cooling.

Production of laminated croissant pastry sample recipe

Method:

> ➢ Disperse yeast, sugar and egg in water
>
> ➢ Add liquid to the flour and mix to a dough

Dough Stage: Sieve the flour, milk powder and the salt together, rub the butter into the flour. The dough should be mixed on a 20-quart Hobart-type mixing machine using a dough hook attachment. Mixing times of 2 minutes on 1st speed and 6 minutes on 2nd speed is recommended (Yankellow, 2005). But as always, different flour characteristics will determine mixing times. The shorter mixing time of this dough allows for the shearing action which the dough will encounter when final processing through the pastry sheeter or with a rolling pin is given to the dough. The mixed dough should be kneaded into a ball, placed into a container which will allow for the expansion of the dough during the cold fermentation process and sealed tight or covered with plastic to prevent skinning (Yankellow, 2005). The dough should be fermented for 45 minutes at room temperature, rolled into a rectangle, covered in plastic followed by overnight fermentation in a fridge at a temperature of 3-6 °C (Vernet, 2020).

Base Croissant Recipe

Ingredients	1 Mix	1/2 Mix	Based on flour 100% Bakers %	Hydration %
	Kg / g	Kg / g	500	50.00
Overnight dough Stage 1				
Strong Flour	500	250	100.0 %	
Egg	50	25	10.0 %	
Water	200	100	40.0 %	
Sugar	45	23	9.0 %	
Fresh yeast	35	18	7.0 %	
Milk powder	25	13	5.0 %	
Salt	7	4	1.4 %	
Butter	25	13	5.0 %	
Dough head weight	887	444	**Butter on Dough %**	**Total Butter % in both Dough & Lamination**
Lamination dough Stage 2				
Laminating butter	225	113	25.4	30.4
Total Batch weight	1,112	556		
Yield	15	7		
Scaling wt in grams	75			

Lesson #1 the 3-4-3 system

Pros and cons of pastry made on this system: 25 layers, very flaky externally, very open leafy honeycomb internal texture. It is the easiest of the three systems explained in this book to laminate by hand due to the smaller quantity of layers, and least resistance developed in the folding process. This system is less elastic than a **3-4-4**; **5-4-3** or **3-3-3-3** system.

Process:

The fermented dough is then degassed by sheeting it through a pastry sheeter set to 10-12 mm thickness, wrapped in plastic to prevent skinning, and placed in a freezer to stiffen the dough and chill it close to 0°C for 30 minutes (Vernet, 2020). The dough is then taken from the freezer and formed into an even rectangle twice the size of the butter block. The butter block is placed in the centre of the dough rectangle as illustrated in Figure 9, and the centre is sealed by pinching the dough together, leaving the ends exposed with butter showing at each end.

The lock-in 3

At this stage, the pastry contains three layers, two dough layers on the top and bottom, with the butter layer at the centre. The dough to the sides of the pastry block can also be sliced to ease the processing and is referred to as the sandwich method. The first stage of this process is known as the "Lock-in"; the butter is locked in between two layers of dough (see Figure 9).

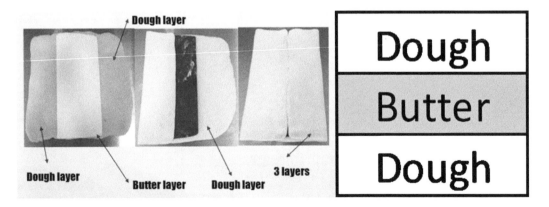

Figure 9: Lock-in sequence, the first 3 layers

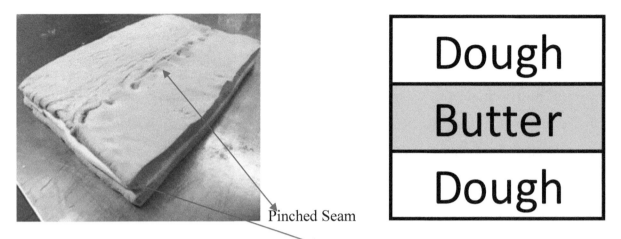

Pinched Seam

Figure 10: The sandwich method the ends are sliced to ease elastic tension of the pastry

The following example explains how a lock-in **3**, followed by a 4-fold determines the number of layers developed by lamination and emphasises the need to factor in the dough contact points. Figure 10 above shows the sandwich method of incorporating dough as a **3** to form the lock-in before sheeting. The pastry is first sheeted/rolled down to approx. 3-3.5mm and folded into a 4-fold, which is offset to one side (4mm x 4 folds = 16mm pastry block height).

Figure 11: Sheeting the lock-in 3

The 4-fold

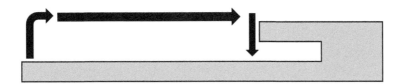

Figure 12: An offset 4-fold noting the open and closed ends of the pastry block

During sheeting, the shaded areas/the dough touching points compress and form one layer of dough as illustrated in Figure 13 below, and therefore the need to subtract one layer for each dough contact point to calculate the actual layers.

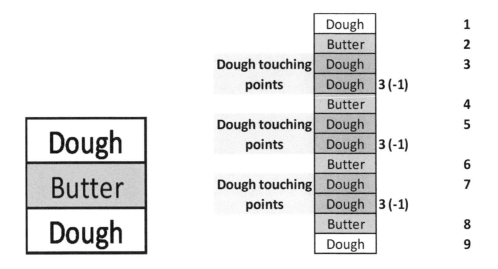

Figure 13: 9 layers formed following sheeting and 4-fold

Figure 14: Sheeted pastry before folding

The 3-fold

The 9 layers formed so far in the process are sheeted out once more to 5mm and then given a 3-fold-3 x9 = 27 (-2 DTP) = 25 Layers, illustrated by photos and diagram in Figure 15 below. The pastry block will be approximately 15mm thick (3-fold x 5mm thick= 15mm).

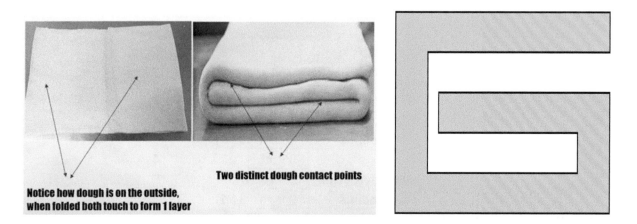

Figure 15: Final 3-fold in the 3-4-3 lamination sequence

The pastry block now has 25 alternating layers of dough and butter and should be pinned out to between 12mm - 15mm, wrapped in plastic and chilled for 30-45 min in a freezer or between ice blankets to relax the gluten and control the temperature of the pastry.

Pastry sheeter settings

Figure 16: Calibration settings on a pastry sheeter (Rondo, n.d.)

Pastry sheeters or reversible sheeters are used worldwide to make the laminated pastry. The dough or pastry is reduced down to a specific thickness on each fold sequence using a reduction wheel which is calibrated numerically in millimetres from 30mm down to 1mm. Larger machines have more comprehensive settings 45mm or more, but usually, it will be the smaller numbers which are mostly in general use. There is normally a locking adjustment to pre-set the rollers to a gap in mm. When using this function, the pastry will remain at the pre-set thickness programmed into the sheeter setting. It will not sheet any thinner, both preventing the operator sheeting too thinly, and giving the pastry a predetermined sheeting thickness for consistency.

Lock-in and first sheeting settings overview

My advised sheeter settings for making laminated pastry are as follows: The block of pastry should be reduced as follows, descending in units of 5 to 10mm, then smaller increments from 10mm downwards as the pastry gets thinner. Ensure the stop has been engaged to prevent the pastry from being pinned too thinly.

- ➤ 30 mm
- ➤ 25 mm
- ➤ 20 mm
- ➤ 15 mm
- ➤ 10 mm
- ➤ 7 mm
- ➤ 3 - 4 mm then fold as required

Reducing the pastry block to this thickness ensures that the butter is correctly incorporated between the two layers of dough. The pastry should be given either a 3 or 4-fold at this stage. For example, if we give the pastry a 4-fold, the pastry block will be a little over 16 mm (4mm thick x 4 folds) = 16mm, plus the air spaces between. Reset the sheeter to 20mm, rotate the pastry 90° to have the open end facing away from you and the closed-end (the belly) facing your stomach.

Pre-lock-in

I recommend, the **3**-4-3 system to begin pastry production and when you become familiar, you can try other lamination systems of different number systems. The pastry can be hand-laminated at all stages of production. If you are using a sheeter, sheet the dough to approximately 12mm and the butter to 5mm. Then when the lock-in is made, the block of dough will have two dough layers of 12mm, and one of butter of 5 mm thick-28 mm in height, which will easily pass through the sheeter rollers. When hand rolling croissant dough, the height of the pastry is not such an issue for initial sheeting height. Most basic reversible pastry sheeters have rollers which only open out to 30mm, but bigger high capacity sheeters open to 45mm.

Second fold and sheeting settings

The block of pastry should now be a little more than 16mm, hence the setting of 20mm to commence sheeting; allowing for some expansion/relaxation and again the pastry should be reduced through the rollers as follows, descending in units of 5 to 10mm. This time the final sheeter setting should be 5mm as the butter is already well incorporated into the pastry.

- ➢ 20 mm
- ➢ 15 mm
- ➢ 10 mm
- ➢ 7 mm
- ➢ 5 - 6 mm then fold as required

The pastry should be given either a 3 or 4-fold at this stage. For example, if we give the pastry a 3-fold, the pastry block will be a little over 15 mm (5mm thick x 3 folds) = 15mm, plus the air spaces between. Reset the sheeter to 20mm thick, rotate the pastry 90° to have the open end facing away from you and the closed-end (the belly) facing your stomach. Reduce to 12mm and chill in the freezer wrapped in plastic. Rest for 30-40 minutes before sheeting, then the pastry is now ready for sheeting and cutting.

Final sheeting settings

The block of pastry should now be a little more than 12mm after relaxing in the fridge, hence the setting of 15mm to commence sheeting, allowing for dough relaxation/fermentation and again the pastry should be reduced as follows, descending in units of 5 to 10 mm. Then bring it down in settings of 2mm at a time until you arrive at your final setting. The final sheeter setting, or mm thickness should set on the sheeter in advance and the pastry sheeted to whatever thickness is required for your pastries. Once more, ensure the lock is on to prevent pinning the pastry too thinly.

- ➤ 15 mm
- ➤ 10 mm
- ➤ 7 mm
- ➤ 5 mm
- ➤ 4 - 3.5 mm for croissant or whatever thickness is required for an individual pastry.

Lesson #2 the 5-4-3 lamination system

Pros and cons of pastry made on this system:

49 layers, less flaky externally, closer leafy honeycomb internal texture, slightly more difficult to hand laminate due to developed elasticity from creating extra layers. Good eating qualities, not as flaky as the other pastry making systems 3-4-3 or 3-4-4.

Process: The **5**-4-3 system begins by sheeting the chilled dough to a rectangle. The chilled, prepared butter block is then placed over 4/5^{ths} of the dough; the dough is then folded into three, forming two layers of butter and three layers of dough-5 layers. In total This is known as lock-in **5** where the butter is locked into the dough.

The 5 lock-in

- ➤ The first stage is always known as the "Lock-in" stage
- ➤ To fold a lock-in **5,** apply butter over the top 4/5^{ths} of the pinned dough
- ➤ Stretch the dough flap at the bottom to cover 1/2 of the butter block
- ➤ Fold the top third down, and you will have 5 alternating layers, 3 of dough, two of butter.

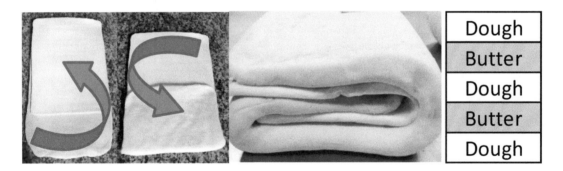

Figure 17: The lock-in 5 with three layers of dough and two layers of butter

The dough is then flattened out using a rolling pin and rolled out thin to between 3.5-4 mm thick using a sheeter or a rolling pin to create a long even strip of pastry which will then be folded into a 4 or a book fold (4mm thick pastry x 4 folds = 16mm pastry block). If hand laminating, it is very important to use dusting flour when rolling and ensure that the pastry never sticks to the work surface, otherwise the layering can be damaged, and the resulting pastry is not of good quality or appearance. .Proceed to the next stage.

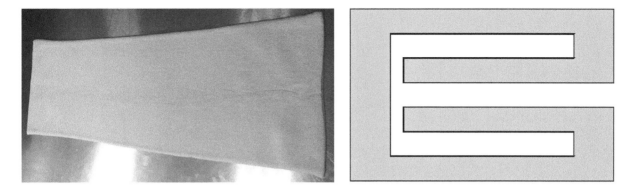

Figure 18: The sheeted pastry to 3.5mm thick and given a 4-fold

The 4-fold

Following the lock-in **5**, the four-fold is the first of two folds after the lock-in **5**, and after the pastry has been sheeted, to between 3.5-4mm thick, and then given the four-fold or a 4.

Procedure:

The pastry block is flattened and rolled or sheeted into a long, thin rectangle of approximately 3.5-4mm. Pinning to this thickness helps ensure that the dough and butter are sheeted together to form a sheet of pastry with 5 distinct, separate layers and then given a book fold, also known as a (4), or a four-fold, This process is achieved by lifting the ends of the pastry, drawing them together towards each other and joining them slightly off centre. The pastry is then folded over like a book, and the pastry has been folded into 4 pleats (see Figure 19). The five combined layers of dough and butter from the **5**-lock-in stage are folded into four pleats, giving the pastry block technically **5** x 4 layers. The pastry block now has 20 (-3 DTP)-17 layers, subtracting one layer each place where the dough touches dough. There are alternate layers of dough and butter. The pastry block should be approximately 16mm high (4mm pastry x 4 folds=16mm height of pastry block) Then sheet the pastry block to between 12-15mm, wrap in plastic to prevent skinning and place in the freezer for 30 minutes, ice blankets may also be used to chill down the pastry. Remember, when you compress two layers of dough together, they merge to become one layer and should be subtracted in the counting of the total quantity of layers.

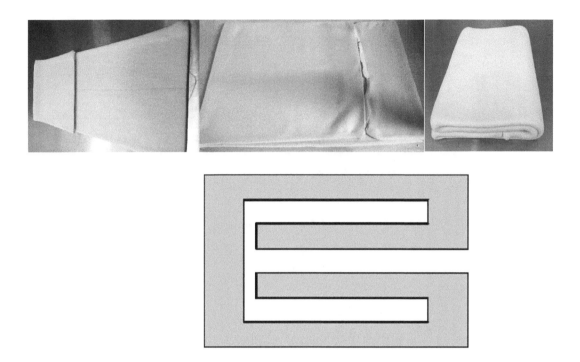

Figure 19: Sheeted pastry block folded into an offset 4-fold with 17 layers.

Freezing and resting

The pastry should be sheeted to between 12-15mm and wrapped in plastic to prevent condensation and freezer burn. The reason for further sheeting to is to thin out the pastry, so the freezer can reduce the core temperature of the pastry block quickly and prevent the yeast from fermenting before the pastry is prepared for final sheeting. When the pastry is folded in this manner above into a 4, there will always be two parts, the outside of the dough touching each or DTP. To calculate the number of layers in the pastry so far, where dough touches dough, it does not count as two separate layers. Remember, when you compress two layers of dough together, they merge to become one layer and should be subtracted in the counting of layers. Therefore, it is counted as one layer. Where this occurs three times in this 4-fold, three DTP are subtracted from the overall number of layers, and the pastry now has 17 layers at this stage in the process, see Figures 20 and 21.

Layer calculation example after subtraction of DTP 4-Fold

	Material		Layers
	Dough		1
	Butter		2
	Dough		3
	Butter		4
Dough touching points	Dough		5
	Dough	5 (-1)	
	Butter		6
	Dough		7
	Butter		8
Dough touching points	Dough		9
	Dough	5 (-1)	
	Butter		10
	Dough		11
	Butter		12
Dough touching points	Dough		13
	Dough	5 (-1)	
	Butter		14
	Dough		15
	Butter		16
	Dough		17

Material	Layers
Dough	1
Butter	2
Dough	3
Butter	4
Dough	5
Butter	6
Dough	7
Butter	8
Dough	9
Butter	10
Dough	11
Butter	12
Dough	13
Butter	14
Dough	15
Butter	16
Dough	17

Figure 20: Layering diagram lock-in 5 and a 4-fold Figure 21: Final layer count

The 3-fold

The croissant pastry is removed from the freezer and placed on the pastry sheeter. The pastry is then rolled to 5mm into a rectangle and folded into 3 (see Figure 21), commonly known as a trifold, a simple fold or a 3. The pastry is now 15mm thick. In this stage of production, the dough has 17 x 3 layers. 51 (-2) where dough touches the dough. The pastry now has 49 separate layers of dough and butter. Wrap in plastic to prevent skinning and place in the freezer for 40 minutes or use ice blankets to chill down the pastry for 30-45 minutes before sheeting.

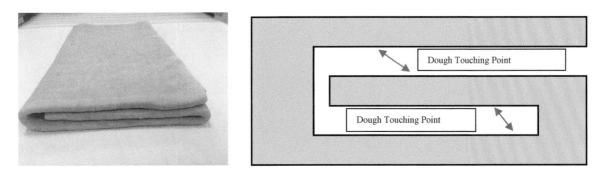

Figure 22: A trifold, letter fold, 3 or a simple fold

The final stage is the sheeting stage. Sheeting effectively is the process of reducing the pastry to the thickness required for final processing (see Figure 23). Sheet the pastry to between 3.5-4 mm and place in freezer for 10-15 min. Process as you desire: croissant, pain au, chocolat, etc.

Figure 23: Sheeting of pastry example

Lamination sequencing 3-4-3: The dough and the butter will have a similar consistency which allows the pastry to be sheeted with ease without sheeting down either the dough layers or the butter. The sheeting of the pastry block followed by folding sequences allows layers of dough and butter to build up simultaneously. As the butter is a fat and the dough is water-based, they will remain separate when they are rolled out during the sheeting process, this allows for the formation of individual layers of dough and butter by folding the pastry in designated sequences. Following the **3** lock-in, the dough now contains three layers, i.e. dough, butter, dough. This is known as the first **3** of the lamination sequences. The pastry is placed on a sheeter and rotated 90° from the formation of the lock-in; the seam formed oriented to point horizontally towards the machine rollers. The thickness of the pastry is gradually reduced by 3mm at a time to a final thickness of 3-4 mm on a pastry sheeter. The pastry should then be given a book fold or a 4-fold, as illustrated in Figure 24 below.

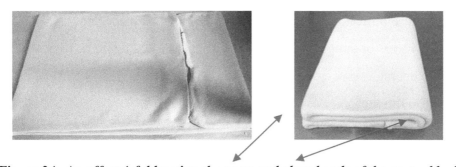

Figure 24: An offset 4-fold noting the open and closed ends of the pastry block

An offset method of folding is recommended, as this reduces the possibility of a bulge in the leading edge of the pastry block, which can result in uneven sheeting. The mechanical friction of the rolling process generates heat and increases the temperature of the pastry. At this stage, it is recommended that the pastry is rotated 90° with the closed seam facing the operator and reduced to a 12mm thickness on the pastry sheeter, wrapped in plastic and placed in a freezer at-18 °C for 20 minutes. The 90° rotation of the pastry ensures that the pastry is stretched in each direction evenly throughout the process (NIIR Board of Consultants and Engineers, 2014), which eliminates shrinkage in the final proofing and baking stages of production. Reducing the pastry to a thickness of 12-15mm enables the freezer to reduce the core temperature of the pastry rapidly, controlling the fermentation until the proofing stage.

As the pastry at lock-in initially had three layers or a **3**, it was sheeted and folded into four or a 4-fold. One would imagine that 3 x 4 would equal 12 layers; however, where dough touches dough in the folding process, known as "The Dough Contact Point" or DCP, one layer is subtracted at each dough contact point. Under compression, the dough merges to form a single dough layer while the butter layer remains unchanged. In the case of a 4-fold, three dough touching/contact points are counted, leaving a total of 9 layers of dough and butter. The chilled pastry is then removed from the freezer for up to 45 minutes for its final sheeting and folding.

Once again, it is essential to rotate the pastry 90° so that the closed seam is facing the operator. The pastry is then sheeted to a thickness of 8-10mm and given a half-fold or a 3. At this stage of the process, the pastry contains 9 x 3 layers or 27 layers. However, as there are two DCPs as seen in Figure 24, two layers are subtracted from the total, and the finished pastry now has a final total of 25 separate alternating layers of dough and butter. The pastry should again be rotated 90°, with the closed end facing the operator, sheeted to a thickness of 12mm, wrapped in plastic and chilled in a freezer at -18°C for 30 minutes.

The sheeting process The pastry is now ready for the preparation of many different types of viennoiserie, such as classic croissant, pain au chocolat or pain aux raisins and can be sheeted down to the required thickness.

Lesson #3 the 3-3-3 / 3 system

Pros and cons of pastry made with this system: 55 layers, less flaky externally than previous systems, closer honeycomb internal texture and good eating qualities, the most elastic of the doughs due to the extra layering, the pastry will shrink when cutting if not well-rested. Takes longer to make because of the additional layers and the additional rest time required in the process.

Process:

The process of lock-in is as in previous pastry making systems, all of which have been well described. I have included additional notes for using and handling coloured or flavoured types of butter just below Figure 27.

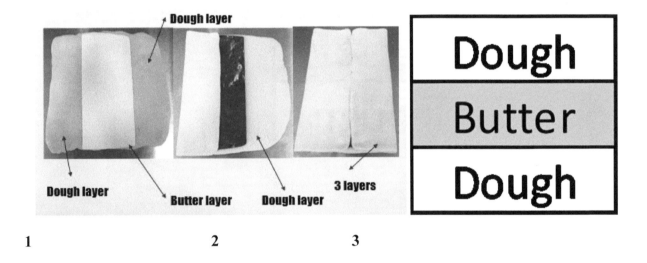

1 2 3

Figure 25: The 3-3-3 / 3 lock in stage

The **3**-3-3 / 3 system begins by sheeting the chilled dough to a rectangle. The dough rectangle is placed on the table in landscape format. The pre-chilled prepared butter block is positioned in the middle of the dough (see Figure 25). Imagine, for example, like the Irish flag, the dough rectangle is presented in landscape form. The butter block is placed in the middle of the dough rectangle. Next, the dough is folded over the butter to the centre.

The two edges of the dough are pressed together in the centre, as shown in Figure 26. There are now two layers of dough and one layer of butter - the three layers.

The lock-in 3

Figure 26: Preparing lock-in 3

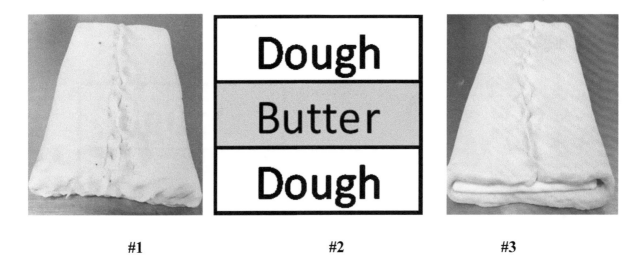

#1   #2   #3

Figure 27: Lock in with pastry folded over and open on the right

Note: In the photos above Figure 27, the ends are sealed on the #1dough on the left, as there is chocolate butter inside. Sealing the butter entirely inside the dough protects the belts on the pastry sheeter from being soiled by the chocolate butter. If making plain croissant pastry, the ends should not be sealed as in #3 above. Alternatively, the sides can be cut with a sharp knife or pizza wheel and exposed, known as the Sandwich Method, (see Figure 28) ensuring that no large masses of dough are present in the finished pastry and that the butter is evenly distributed between the formed layers.

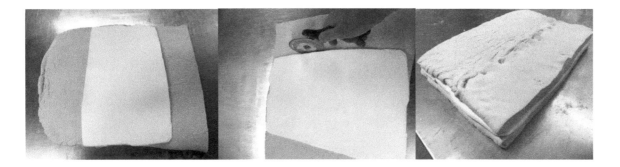

Figure 28: The sandwich method – butter exposed on all sides

The pastry block above is rolled into a rectangle 3.5-4mm thick and given a trifold, or a **3**. The pastry now has 3 x 3= 9 layers (-2 DTP) or 7 separate layers of dough and butter. The pastry is sheeted a second time to 5mm given another trifold or 3. The folded pastry now has 3 x 7=21 layers (-2 DTP) or 19 alternating layers of pastry. The pastry block should be rolled down to 12-15mm. Wrapped in plastic and placed in the freezer for 30 minutes or use Ice blankets.

The pastry is then taken from the freezer and is rolled to 5mm into a long rectangle and folded into 3. The pastry now has 3 x 19 layers = 57 (-2 DTP) or 55 layers. The 12-15mm thickness of the pastry block helps achieve a low core temperature in the freezer swiftly. The pastry can now be either processed or frozen for up to four weeks at-18°C at this stage. If freezing, seal in plastic and freeze to -18°C When required, remove the frozen pastry block and place in a fridge @3-4°C the evening before you need it, to defrost overnight in the fridge. Then sheet the pastry the following morning, cut, proof and bake. If processing the pastry straight away, sheet the pastry to 3.5-4 mm and place in freezer for 10-15 minutes, this prevents shrinking of the pastry. Process as you desire, croissant, pain au chocolat, or other varieties.

Overview of the 3-3-3-3 system, lock-in, sheeting and first trifold

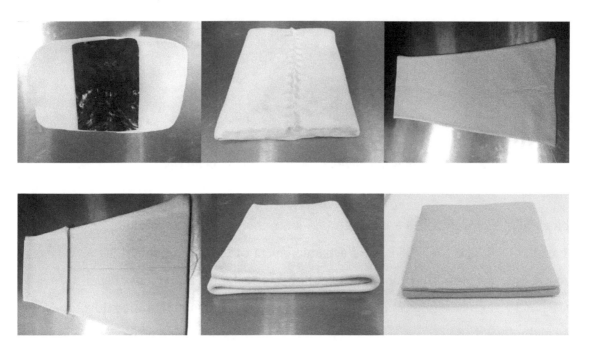

Figure 29: Recap lock in and first trifold

There are many pastry folding combinations; I have just covered three systems here, two involving three folds **3**-4-3; and **5**-4-3, the other with four folds **3**-3-3-3. Here's an overview of what has been covered and a mention of other systems. The lock-in number will always be the first number. The optimum thickness per layer is 0.08-0.10mm. Applying this formula to the layers below, the sheeting thickness can be calculated using a thickness size of 0.08mm per layer.

The lock in 5 series of layering:

Lamination system	Layers	Sheeting Thickness (Layersx0.08mm)	Product type
5-4-4	65	5.2 mm	Single piece cut pastry
5-5-3	61	4.88 mm	Large croissant
5-3-4	52	4.16 mm	Medium to large croissant
5-4-3	49	3.92 mm	Large croissant >120g
5-3-3	37	2.96 mm	Pain au Chocolat
5-5-2	41	3.28 mm	Medium croissant

The lock in 3 series of layering

Lamination system	Layers	Sheeting Thickness (Layersx0.08mm)	Product type
3-3-3-3	55	4.4 mm	Large croissant
3-5-4	41	3.28 mm	Medium croissant
3-4-5	41	3.28 mm	Medium croissant
3-4-4	33	2.64 mm	Pain au Chocolat
3-4-3	25	2.0 mm	Large layered pastry
3-3-4	25	2.0 mm	Two merged pastry 50 layers
3-3-3	19	1.52 mm	Outer layer for merged pastry
3-4-2	18	1.44 mm	Twin lamination option 2 x 18 layers 36 layers- 1 DTP , 35 layers

Processing notes recap for the lamination 3-3-3-3

➢ Lock-in the butter as a **3** over the centre of the dough. Sheet to 4mm

➢ Trifold #1 (3 layers) that we give the pastry also referred to as the second 3 in the sequence

➢ Trifold #2 (3 layers), is given straight after the first; rotate the pastry block 90° to have the seam on the side. Sheet to 5mm, fold and sheet again to 12mm, wrap in plastic, place in freezer for 20-30 minutes

➢ Trifold #3 (3 layers), sheet to 5mm rotate pastry block 90° to have the seam facing you

➢ The pastry is now made and needs time to recover from sheeting

➢ Sheet to 12mm wrap in plastic, place in freezer 20-30 minutes or place between ice blankets

➢ Sheet the pastry to 3.5-4 mm and chill again before cutting out for 5-10 min in the freezer

➢ Ideally, leave the finished pastry for 30 minutes in the freezer at-18°C before final sheeting

Keeping count of the number of folds made on the pastry

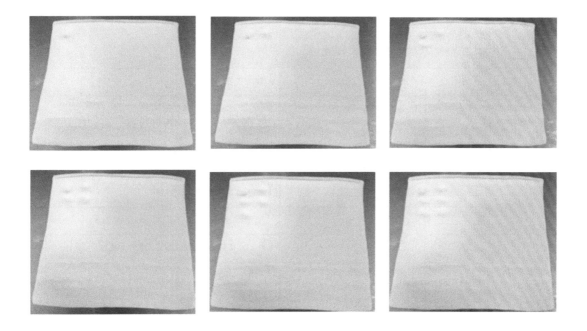

Figure 30: Indenting pastry to track the number of folds

A simple indentation made with your finger following each fold of the pastry will remind you at what stage you are at in the production of the pastry block. This system also works well if there is more than one person in the bakery or pastry kitchen making the pastry together, on a production line, for example. The illustration above was made giving puff paste six single turns.

Recommended layering for different pastry sizes/weight

Croissant: 5-4-3,   3-4-3   or   3-3-3-3;   **Chocolatine:**   3-4-4

The more layers, the tighter the pastry, the smaller number of layers, the flakier the pastry will be, remember, the yeast will rise the dough component of the pastry also and generate lift in the oven. Larger pastries require a greater number of layers to support the increased mass.

Processing the pastry - rolling out the croissants

Calculating the final thickness of sheeting out the pastry can be measured and decided in advance by allowing an optimum thickness of 0.08mm for each individual layer formed while making pastry. By counting the number of total layers formed when creating the pastry, for example, the 49 layers formed in the **5-4-3** system; or the 55 layers formed in the **3-3-3-3** system.

0.08mm x 49 (layers from 5-4-3- system) = Sheeting thickness of 3.92mm

0.08mm x 55 (layers from 3-3-3-3-system) = Sheeting thickness of 4.40mm

➢ Sheet to between 3.5- 4.4 mm or as required.

➢ Cut the pastry into triangles as demonstrated and at the bottom in the middle with a large French knife, or simply roll the end slightly thinner to elongate the base of the croissant place the triangles in the freezer for 10-15 min to arrest fermentation and prevent shrinkage

➢ They should weigh between 65-75g, make an incision in the middle of the base of the triangle

➢ The croissants should be slightly stretched to resemble the Eiffel Tower in shape

➢ They can also be rolled on the base with a thin rolling pin to make the foot wider

➢ Roll out gently, not tight, from the bottom in an outward motion

➢ The croissant should freely open if held at the top and released

Figure 31: Eiffel Tower shape of croissant before rolling

Croissant and chocolatine cutting guide table

All measurements are a personal choice, some people prefer to work with very long triangles, for croissant, others like fewer coils or feet, the guide below will assist the production of a variety of sizes pastries from large, to mini for breakfast buffets. All measurements are a guide, lengths may be increased as desired. Croissant triangle ratio of 1 : 3; Pain au Chocolat rectangle ratio of 1: 1.5

Croissant measurements   Triangle ratio 1: 3

	Width	Length	Thickness
	cm	cm	mm
Large	10	30	3.5 - 4
	9	27	3.5 - 4
	8	24	3.5 - 4
	7	21	3.5 - 4
	6	18	3.5 - 4
	5	15	3.5 - 4

Chocolatine measurements   Rectangle ratio 1:1.5

	Width	Length	Thickness
	cm	cm	mm
Large	10	15	3.5 - 4
	9	13.5	3.5 - 4
	8	12	3.5 - 4
	7	10.5	3.5 - 4
	6	9	3.5 - 4
	5	7.5	3.5 - 4

Figure 32: Cutting size ratios for croissant and pain au chocolat

Egg washing and proofing

Egg wash recipe:

Two eggs

One egg yolk

Pinch of salt

> The addition of salt to the egg wash helps to breakdown the chalazae, which hold the yolk in place in the egg; giving a more homogeneous mix and uniform egg wash with no lumps of tissue in the wash.

➢ Proof @26-27°C with 75% to 80% relative humidity. It is important not to proof any hotter as the butter layers will melt and run out of the dough if the temperature exceeds 28°C

➢ Proofing time will always depend on temperature, amount of yeast and humidity

➢ Proof time 1.5 to 2 hours +. You will know they are proofed when the layers visually begin to separate. Also, the "Wobble Test" by shaking the tray gently, the proofed croissants should wobble like jelly

➢ When egg washing pastry, use a very soft artist's paintbrush to apply the egg wash

➢ Always take care not to brush the cut edges of the pastry with egg as this will reduce its final volume

Baking temperature factors

➢ Having the oven at the correct working temperature is essential

➢ The preferred oven type for pastry is a fan or convection oven, however, using a deck oven requires a slightly hotter baking temperature setting of 200°C with a heat intensity setting of 6 on top, 6 on the bottom and 6 at the door. The oven should be 10-20°C hotter before loading, and the temperature reset after filling the oven with product and trays

- ➤ The fan oven should be set at 220°C to allow a temperature drop of approximately 50°C during loading of the oven before baking
- ➤ After loading the fan oven, drop the temperature to between 170-175°C depending on the oven type, and the size of the pastry, as each oven has its individual characteristics. The pastries should be baked for 14-20 min with a little steam

After baking - care of pastry

- ➤ Allow the pastries to cool fully on the tray before moving them.
- ➤ When cool, do not stack pastry items one on top of the other as they will collapse.
- ➤ Store in airtight containers if not on display for sale to extend shelf life

The almond twice-baked croissant

To make these delicious twice baked croissants, follow the recipe overleaf on page 77.

Almond cream recipe

Leftover croissants can be made into almond croissants and are a great way of using up leftovers. Cream the butter and sugar with the almonds and flour until fluffy, add the egg over three additions. Leftover croissants are cut in half, the crumb brushed with rum syrup, piped with almond cream, and the top is piped with more almond cream, then dipped into almond flakes. The almond croissants are baked then for 15 -20 minutes at 180°C, allowed to cool and then dredged in icing sugar. If dusted when still warm, the icing sugar will turn yellow and does not look as attractive.

500g	Butter	500g	Castor sugar
70g	Pastry flour	500g	Ground almonds
450g	Egg	20g	Almond essence

Method

Cream butter, flour, sugar and almonds until fluffy. Add the egg and almond essence over three additions.

Rum syrup recipe

100g sugar; 100g water; boil, allow to cool, then add 10g red rum and brush into croissant crumb. Store in the fridge when not in use.

Twin lamination croissant and chocolate croissant pastry

Always fascinated by pastry since I was a child; I had a burning desire and curiosity to push the boundaries of my knowledge. My dear deceased father and mentor Anthony Griffin, RIP introduced me to lamination and taught me the principles of pastry as a young man. He would never realise the effect of his influence and tuition in our small family bakery in Galway, Ireland would have on my life and career as a baker. I knew that I needed to give myself time and immerse myself in an environment away from work, where I could focus on my creativity. In 2016, that itch was scratched, I bit the bullet. I decided to enrol as a mature student in the one - year masters' degree level 9 program at the Dublin Institute of Technology (now Technological University Dublin). The masters' degree was of Food Product Development and Culinary Innovation at the School of Culinary Arts and Food Technology. One of the many modules for completion was to develop a totally new product with market potential, something never made before, so I came up with the idea of a twin laminated pastry. I was always a big fan of world-class baker David Bedu. David is the creator of the iconic bicolor croissant. We served as jury members together in Casablanca 2019 at the African Bakery Cup. I took his creation one step further, and, where his iconic pastry was a block of croissant pastry with a chocolate brioche top; I decided to conduct my research into developing a twin laminated pastry with a laminated chocolate pastry merged with plain croissant pastry. My choice of project was because, while I adored the aspect and appearance of the bicolor croissant, I found that the outside layer of chocolate brioche used in bicolor croissant production made the pastry less flaky. For me, the flakier the pastry, the more I enjoy it. If it doesn't make a flaky mess on my plate when I'm eating it, I am not fully satisfied, as I love the crunchy mouthfeel and texture that is unique only to a well-made laminated pastry. I decided to turn my attention and investigate making a laminated chocolate pastry and merge it with standard croissant pastry, double the layers, double the enjoyment and the mess! That was my inspiration and vision for the twin laminated pastry which I went on to produce for my masters' degree practical in innovative product production. I used the time to experiment and tried well over 100 combinations of pastry lamination, but I learned a lot from the studies and graduated my MSc. with first class honours, as student of the year with the highest academic mark and won the Stafford Lynch award 2016.

Preparing chocolate flavored butter for twin lamination

The critical differences in twin laminated pastry over bicolor pastry are the preparation of two separate laminated pastries which are then merged together and processed as one block of pastry. Chocolate butter is prepared by mixing cocoa and butter slowly together on a machine with a cake beater. The butter and cocoa powder are mixed until combined to form chocolate butter. The butter is then made into a butter block and chilled down to 3°C before lamination.

Figure 33: Preparing chocolate butter

Base recipes for croissant pastry production

The base croissant recipe will successfully make the most delicious laminated pastry. Many variations can be made by altering the butter flavours with cocoa powder, instant coffee, raspberry powder, strawberry powder, orange and lemon rind and seaweed. Double the dough recipe, prepare two different kinds of butter, there are infinite choices, but these are my own findings.

Twin lamination pastry with spelt flour

Stage 1: Making two different types of classic laminated pastry from one dough

- ➢ Croissant pastry - where the butter is added, and the pastry is laminated
- ➢ Chocolate croissant pastry - chocolate butter is added, and the pastry is laminated.

Figure 34: Chocolate and plain croissant pastry

Stage 2:   45 minutes of room temperature fermentation, followed by overnight fermentation in a fridge @3°C

Stage 3:   Lamination process of layering the butter into the plain spelt croissant dough using various lamination techniques and sequences

Stage 4:   Lamination process of layering the chocolate butter into the spelt croissant dough using various lamination techniques and sequences

Stage 4.   Merging of the two types of pastry together

Stage 5.   Lamination, cutting and formation of individual pastry pieces

Stage 6:   Proofing of the products 90-120 minutes @25-27°C and 75%-80% RH

Stage 7:   Baking of the products @170-175-°C for 15-20 minutes (rack oven); 200°C (deck oven)

Method:

Remove the croissant dough from the fridge and process as below, adding the chocolate butter to one of the doughs at stage 1. Process as per stage 5 instructions. Both doughs require similar lamination numbers for the desired layer quantities.

Dough #1- For the chocolate dough:

Chocolate Dough	Stages	Instructions 3-3-3-Lamination system- 19 layers
Lamination stages:	Stage 1	Lock in the chocolate butter using a "3" then pin to 5-6mm
	Stage 2	Make a trifold (3) layers pin to 7-8mm
	Stage 3	Make a trifold (3) layers pin to 12mm then freezer 30 minutes
	Stage 4	Pin dough and place over the laminated plain croissant dough

Dough # 2 - For the plain dough

Plain Dough	Stages	Instructions 3-3-3 Lamination system 19 layers
Lamination stages:	Stage 1	Lock in the butter using a "3", pin to 5 mm
	Stage 2	Make a trifold (3) layers pin to 7-8mm,
	Stage 3	Make a trifold (3) layers pin to 7-8 mm then to freezer 30 min
	Stage 4	Place underneath the laminated chocolate croissant dough

Dough # 3 - Merge the chocolate and plain doughs together and process as below:

Details Sheeting:	Stages	Instructions:
Sheeting the pastry:	Stage 5	Moisten the pastry using a spray bottle of water. Place chocolate dough on top of plain dough, sheet together
Thickness:		Pin pastry to 3.5-4mm-chill in the freezer for 20-30 minutes
Shape:	Stage 6 Proofing Stage 7 baking	Mark with dividers and cut with a French knife Triangles 10x30cm for Croissant Rectangles 8x15cm for Pain Chocolat
Final proof time:	90-120 min	Maximum of 27.5°C 85% RH. Egg wash before baking
Baking temperature:	185°C-200°C	
Baking time:	15-18 min	

Mixing stage plain or spelt croissant dough # 1

Stage	Ingredients	Kg/g	Method
1	T55 or Spelt Flour Salt Butter	1010 20 32	Mix flour & salt together in a 10qt Hobart mixer Use the dough hook attachment Add the butter
2	Milk fresh Water Sugar Milk powder Yeast Malt	258 258 121 26 66 2	Disperse yeast, dry milk powder and sugar in the water/milk Use a hand whisk to blend and add all to stage 1 Mix the dough for 4 minutes on slow-4 minutes on 2nd speed Mix ingredients to a stiff dough. Cover with plastic
	Total:	1793	Ferment at room temperature 45 min Set aside in refrigerator overnight @ 3˚C 12-18hours
3	Butter Dry 84%	500	Prepare butter for lamination as demonstrated in the YouTube videohttps://youtu.be/Cj0gEXtXexw
	Total:	2293	

Mixing stage chocolate croissant dough #2

Stage	Ingredients	Kg/g	Method
1	T-55 or Spelt Flour Salt Butter	1010 20 32	Mix flour & salt together in a 10qt Hobart mixer Use the dough hook attachment Add the butter
2	Milk fresh Water Sugar Milk powder Yeast Malt	268 268 121 26 66 2	Disperse yeast, dry milk and sugar in the water/milk. Use a hand whisk to blend and add all to stage 1. Mix the dough for 4 minutes on slow-4 minutes on 2nd speed Mix ingredients to a stiff dough, Cover with plastic
	Total:	1793	Ferment at room temperature 45 minutes. Set aside in refrigerator overnight @3˚C for 12-18 hours
3	Dry butter 84% Cocoa	500 75	Prepare butter for lamination. Mix on a machine and prepare butter block as demonstrated in the YouTube video. https://youtu.be/Cj0gEXtXexw
	Total:	2368	

Examples of twin laminated dough and makeup

Figure 35: Croissant dough with chocolate and plain butter

When using two different types of laminated dough, together, the optimum result was achieved by using the following combination of lamination sequences to both individually coloured doughs separately and then merging them both together:

#1 using the – **3**-3-3 sequence of laminating for the white laminated dough (19 layers)
#2 using the – **3**-3-3 sequence of laminating for the laminated chocolate dough (19 layers)
19+19 =38   (-1 DTP) Total 37 layers

My research into pastry has found that the combined sequences above give 37 layers of pastry and are the most appropriate systems for all types of twin merged laminated pastry. Always remember to place the chocolate or coloured/flavoured dough face down on the table when cutting, then when processed, the coloured pastry will be on the outside of the combined pastry after processing.

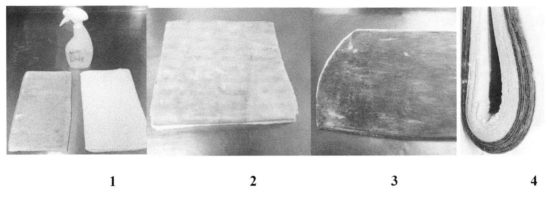

1   2   3   4

Figure 36: Merging the two doughs

The sheeted doughs are measured, sprayed or brushed with a little water to make one surface sticky; then both are pressed together with a rolling pin, to form one block of pastry. They should be gently rolled together on each side to ensure cohesion before sheeting. The pastry can then be sheeted and cut into the various shapes, and fillings of choice such as chocolate bars and/or candied orange peel added.

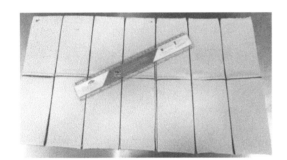 

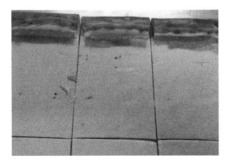

Figure 37: The pastry is measured, cut and fillings applied

Figure 38: The pastry is moulded into shape and placed in the proof cabinet

Figure 39: The proofed pastries

To ensure the pastry is fully/correctly proofed before baking, there are visual clues which indicate when the pastry is ready to bake. The first visual clue is when air spaces appear between the layers of the pastry running right through the pastry from the outside to the core. Remember, that the core of the pastry is where the temperature takes the longest to be penetrated by the heat of the proofer. If not correctly proofed, the pastry will have a dense, gummy core. Viennoiserie will always proof from the outside to the centre. Coiled and high pastry such as croissant and pain au chocolat will always take at least two hours to proof under normal proof conditions (26-27°C). Coiled, but flatter pastries, such as pain aux raisins, cinnamon rolls or those cut with cutters, such as the pear pastries page 134 will proof faster as they are not as thick or high. Correct proofing is very important for establishing a delightful honeycomb interior, and it is the holy grail of viennoiserie making. Pay particular attention to the innermost fold, the start of your pain au chocolat coil in the very centre, if there is good separation, you are nearly there.

Figure 40: Layer separation air spaces

The "Wobble Test" also known as "The Bay Watch Shake" is the other visual clue where, when the tray is gently shaken, the entire pastry quivers like a bowl of jelly. I attach a link on YouTube where this test may be viewed. Wobble Test: click the link - http://youtu.be/czyabhubp1k pain au chocolat "Wobble" Test (Griffin, 2016).

Figure 41: Examples of chocolate and plain merged laminated spelt dough

A YouTube video showing some of the above pastries being baked on time-lapse is available on the link below. Chocolatine baking in a time-lapse movie (Griffin, 2016)

Click link for time-lapse video http://youtu.be/-yvqngzw3gs

The double chocolate chocolatine

The double chocolate twin laminated pastry is a chocolatine, coiled style pastry made with two types of laminated croissant pastry pinned together to a thickness of 3.5mm, see Figure 36 and page 83-84. Two croissant bars are used inside the pastry as is typical for chocolatine, and the pastry can be dusted with dark cocoa or icing sugar after cooling. To make an even crispier pastry, this one is typically scored several times before rolling. The layers open out during the proof stage and increase the surface area of crispy layers.

Bicolor croissants and pain au chocolat 3-4-4

Figure 42: Bicolor chocolate croissant and chocolatine

My dear friend French master baker David Bedu, based in Florence, Italy, was the creator of the "Croissant Bicolor." He inspired me to both mimic and recreate his legendary croissant in a different and unique form. The croissant bicolor is the fusion of a croissant dough block before sheeting with a coloured sheet of brioche. In David Bedu's case, his iconic chocolate bicolor was created using a cocoa flavoured brioche which covered croissant dough. There have since been countless variations of the bicolor croissant which include strawberry, raspberry, coffee, purple or blue raspberry, green apple to mention but a few. Chocolatines also look very pretty when made using bicolour pastry, especially when scored as above in Figure 42.

To make a nice croissant bicolor chocolate; the white croissant pastry is laminated by using the **3-4-4** sequence. Chocolate brioche is sheeted separately at a ratio of 4:1 or 225g of chocolate yeasted brioche dough per kg of croissant dough. The brioche dough was coloured by the addition of dark cocoa powder at a rate of 10% flour at the mixing stage. This chocolate dough is then sheeted and placed on top of the plain croissant dough before final sheeting, and the combined dough and brioche is then reduced to 3.5mm by passing it through the dough sheeter several times. In the chapter Coupe du Monde Chocolatine,

I have a recipe for chocolate dough using the croissant dough you are making, and it saves time, not having to weigh a separate dough each time you make it (CDMC recipe page 124).

Figure 43: Strawberry red brioche dough applied to croissant dough before sheeting

Many unique products can be made using a combination of bicolor croissant dough and with the addition of fillings and flavours which complement the chocolate, such as orange, mint and raspberry. When colouring brioche dough, I recommend the use of dry powder or edible paste colours which should be added at the beginning of the mixing. Paste and powder colours retain most of their colour following the baking process. There are also many choices of natural concentrated food colours for making this type of pastry on the market today.

Figure 44: Raspberry bicolor croissant

The orange chocolate bicolor chocolatine 5-4-3

The orange chocolate bicolor is made using 250g of chocolate brioche per 1 kg of croissant dough. The dough is merged with the chocolate brioche and sheeted to 3.5-4mm. The pastry is cut 15cm long x 8cm wide with the chocolate brioche side of the pastry face down on the table. The chopped pieces are brushed with a minimal amount of orange oil and rolled up with two chocolate bars and a slice of candied orange peel. The pastry is proofed and baked, allowed to cool and garnished with a half of a candied orange slice.

The cross-laminated croissant and chocolatine

Two-tone, three-tone or four-tone pastry can be made up using the techniques mentioned earlier. In the case of a cross-laminated single colour, for example, a chocolate croissant dough is made using coloured butter and a smaller number of layers the **3**-3-3 system. The pastry is then frozen in a block and when semi-hard, it is sliced into strips, and the strips are placed facing up on top of a chilled plain croissant block of dough until the dough is entirely covered. The block of pastry is then sheeted, ensuring that the layers on the top of the block are stretched to elongate them and not widen the layers as this will lose the effect of cross lamination.

Examples of cross lamination techniques

Figure 45: Chocolate cross lamination New York with Peter Yuen 2015

Figure 46: Strawberry butter is made up and incorporated into the pastry

Using 10% freeze-dried fruit powders, a range of flavoured butter such as raspberry, blackberry and mango can be prepared and add exceptional colour and flavour to the pastry. Simply add 10g freeze-dried fruit powder per 100g of lamination butter used in your recipes. Place in a stand mixer with beater attachment, mix on slow to incorporate and make a butter block as normal.

Figure 47: The pastry is laminated 3-4 and then merged

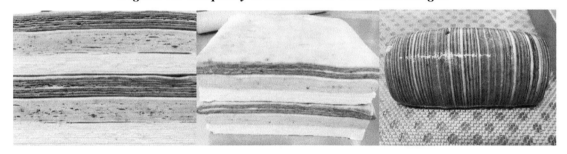

Figure 48: The three colours are laminated and merged

Two-tone or three tone pastry can be made up using the techniques mentioned earlier. The pastry is merged together and frozen. The frozen pastry is removed from the freezer and sliced into strips of 5mm thick, which are placed onto a block of croissant dough. The dough is then sheeted in the same direction as the cut, exposed, layers; taking care only to elongate the layers and not widen them when sheeting the pastry.

 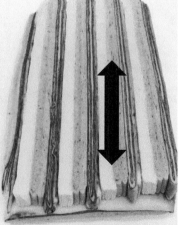

The pastry should be rolled in the direction of the arrow, with the flow of the cut layers, otherwise the layers will widen instead of elongating and the cross-lamination effect will be lost.

Figure 49: Cross lamination three colours

The orange chocolate twin laminated chocolatine

Inspired by David Bedu, I developed this new concept in 2015/2016; twin laminated pastry during my master's degree studies. The orange chocolate croissant is a pain au chocolat-type pastry made using two different types of laminated dough which are merged together before final sheeting. A plain croissant dough and also one made using chocolate butter. The plain croissant dough is laminated using the **3**-3-3 system, and the chocolate croissant dough is made using the **3**-3-3 laminating system. Both doughs are merged together and sheeted to 4mm, giving 37 layers, see page 83.

The pastry is placed on the worktable with the chocolate side down and then cut into rectangles 15cm longx8cm wide. The pastry is brushed with a tiny amount of orange oil and a chocolate croissant bar. I also use candied orange peel strips to enhance the flavour. The candied orange slices are used to garnish the pastry when cool. The orange strips can be made at home, there are plenty of online resources such as Epicurious with step by step instructions on how to make them at home. https://www.epicurious.com/recipes/food/views/simple-candied-orange-peel-350798 also, slices are available commercially from Keylink Ltd in the UK see Page (165 & 166). The candied orange bars are a filling designed to enhance the flavour of the product. They are added before baking for flavouring purposes. They are a natural product, free of sulphides.

The lye dipped croissant 3-3-3

Figure 50: Lye croissant 3-3-3 system

Another interesting variation of the croissant is a lye croissant. If used as a savoury item, adjustments to the recipe can be made by reducing the sugar levels in the recipe by 80%. Lye is also known as Sodium Hydroxide (NaOH) and as a baking application is used to produce pretzels and lye rolls. Lye products are popular in Germany and across Europe. Lye croissants are another variant which may be explored as an option for a different pastry by bakers already using lye.

The croissant is processed in the usual manner; and when ¾ proofed, the croissants are placed into a freezer, or a blast chiller for 10-15 minutes until the outside is frozen solid and the product can be handled without collapsing. A 1:10 solution of reduced food grade lye or NaOH is prepared while the croissants are in the freezer.

Using proper safety equipment to include safety goggles, plastic bib apron, and elbow-length rubber gloves, the frozen croissants are dipped into the lye, allowed to drip on a wire tray before being placed onto baking sheets lined with baking parchment. The croissants should be sprinkled with rock salt, or shaved salt to distinguish them from other products. The lye croissants are then baked as normal, and the baking process removes the harmful lye through a chemical reaction between the heat of the oven and the NaOH. Lye croissants have a rich chestnut colour exposing the paler white layers of pastry in contrast to the accelerated Maillard reaction of the lye on the outer skin. They are attractive to look at and make nice savoury canapes.

Figure 51: Lye solution

It is most important to wash all equipment and trays which comes in contact with lye, as the lye will stain clothing and is corrosive to metal. As lye is a known poison, when not in use, it should be stored in a secure area. The dilutions used for making pretzels or lye croissant should also be kept in a secure area in a clearly marked container as being toxic if ingested.

Four colour cross lamination

The Christmas Chocolatine

While working as a jury member in Shanghai, Coupe Louis Lesaffre, November 2019, I was inspired by all the international teams who had so much to contribute especially team Japan, who produced a stunning three coloured, diamond-shaped viennoiserie. I used four colours in my own interpretation of this magnificent pastry. My variation of the pastry was made by colouring three separate doughs red, green, pink, plus a plain dough to create the four-colour effect.

I used bake-stable powdered colour in each dough, the butter was not coloured. I used my recipe Figure 3, page 41. I made a double recipe and divided the dough in half. The large plain dough was laminated 3-4-3 and then rested in the freezer for 35 minutes. Then I divided one dough into four and coloured the dough using food colour, and each of the coloured doughs was laminated 3-4 and stacked on top of each other, chilled for 30 minutes refer to cross lamination on pages 91-92; before cutting in half, stacking one on top of the other to get double the layers for slicing. Then I carefully marked and cut the four-colour dough into 5mm strips.

Figure 52: Four colours stacked and a cross-section of the laminated colours

The multi-coloured cut layers are laid down on the plain dough facing upwards, neatly, and each layer is sprayed with water to help them stick together. The pastry is then sheeted, marked and cut to size.

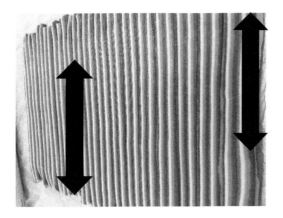

Figure 53: Four colour cross lamination and chocolatines

I cut croissant 10cm wide x 30 cm long; Pain au Chocolate 8cm wide x 15cm long. The arrows above show the direction to sheet the cross-laminated pastry correctly before cutting. I sheeted to 4mm thick I made a variety of chocolatines and croissants from them using chocolate bars, strawberry, and cherry fillings. I have included an instructional video on YouTube on how to make your own home-made chocolate bars, and I used freeze dried strawberry pieces in the chocolate bars to give the pastry some zing. Follow the link below to see the video making the strawberry chocolate bars https://youtu.be/0wMbMnD5ZxY

Figure 54: Four colour chocolatine and croissant

Figure 55: Cross lamination layers and end view of chocolatine

Seaweed croissant

Figure 56: Noribake seaweed blend

I began researching the use of seaweed in and as a food in 2015, by reviewing Japan's consumption of seaweed (the highest, per capita, in the world, with the lowest incidence of obesity and cancer). I introduced new Irish seaweed baked products to customers and colleagues and examined how seaweed could be integrated more efficiently into the western diet. The western diet and food culture differ greatly from that of Asia. So different approaches are required to encourage greater consumption of seaweed which is high in naturally occurring Iodine. Bread and baked products are consumed by most western countries. Adding dried seaweed to flour or in butter for baked goods, or in health drinks, are considered the most appropriate models for achieving this, and indeed yielded encouraging results (Griffin, 2015: ii).

The addition of seaweed to croissant pastry can be achieved in many ways

➢ Added as a dough ingredient

➢ Added to the butter in advance of lamination

➢ Added in a filling after baking

I conducted many test bakes using a product named Noribake (now called Smart Bake) which is available in health food shops nationwide in Ireland, or by contacting the company via their Facebook page of the same name. The seaweed tended to puncture the dough when directly incorporated into it reducing the volume of the croissants in a similar way that wholemeal flour does not yield the same volume as white flour. Following many test bakes, the most beautiful and tasty croissants are made by blending the laminating butter with the seaweed one day before lamination and using a 3-4-3 system.

Figure 57: Seaweed croissant

As seaweed has a strong flavour, the quantity that should be added to the lamination butter should be at 60g per kg of butter. The dried seaweed is simply mixed with the butter in a machine with a beater until blended, then a seaweed butter block is made, chilled and the croissants are made up in the usual manner. The **5**-4-3 laminating sequence also produces an excellent seaweed croissant which is delicious when used with various seafood fillings such as prawn, crabmeat or smoked salmon.

Woodgrain effect croissant 3-4-3

Figure 58: Woodgrain croissant

Woodgrain effect croissants are made by using a combination of a croissant dough block and two yeasted brioche doughs, one plain, one chocolate. The doughs are pinned out thin to a thickness of between 3-4 mm into a neat rectangular sheet. The dough can be sprayed with a fine mist of water, and the two doughs are stuck together and gently rolled with a rolling pin to ensure cohesiveness. The combined dough of chocolate and plain brioche are rolled up tightly into a Swiss roll shape, wrapped tightly in parchment paper and frozen until solid.

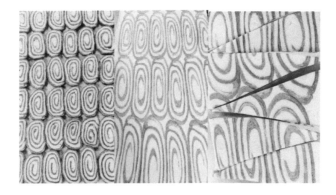

Figure 59: Woodgrain croissant effect using brioche dough

A block of chilled pre-laminated croissant dough, which has yet to be sheeted out is placed on the table and sprayed with a gentle mist of water to enable the brioche dough to stick to it effectively. The frozen brioche dough is then carefully cut into slices of 2-3mm thick discs and placed on top of the croissant pastry, ensuring proper alignment until all the pastry block is covered. The block is then rolled out as normal to produce croissant or pain au chocolat as detailed earlier in the book.

Following the correct procedures for croissant and pain au chocolate, the pastries are shaped and proofed in the usual way as described above. The one difference recommended is that the pastry should be baked in a deck oven for 20 min at a temperature of 200°C. The fan oven gives the pastry too much colour, and the distinction of the wood grain style pastry is not as effective when baked in a fan oven unless baked at a much lower temperature approx.160°C.

Frozen pre-proofed croissants and viennoiserie

Pre proofed frozen croissant and viennoiserie production is the realm of the industrial baker. While I touch on the subject by way of a mention, the process is very scientific, requires expensive equipment /ingredients and uses a lot of energy in production and storage. The recipes supplied in this book can be adjusted to make the pre-proofed frozen pastry by making minor adjustments to the recipes and the process. Pre-proofed frozen pastries by nature require stiffer dough, the moisture content for this type of frozen pastry requires adjustment down to 50% of flour weight or 500g of combined liquid per kg of flour. Specialist bread improvers and yeasts for the freezing process are available on the market. Lesaffre company make a suite of products specifically for this type of frozen production. The addition of dough improver for viennoiserie should be at a dosage recommended by the manufacturer, but usually at 1% of flour weight or 10g per kg of flour. A blast chiller is an essential component in producing pre-proofed frozen croissant dough because of the chiller's ability to reduce the core temperature of the pastry rapidly.

The dough making process is a no-time dough, which is lacking in overnight fermentation to generate flavour, so the addition of up to 20% sourdough to the recipe (see Figure 60) will add flavour to viennoiserie made in this manner, however, adjustments to the recipe are required to balance all the variables, including the quantity of butter used in the final dough. The dough is processed as a no-time dough with a target dough temperature of 20°C is desirable. The mixed dough is given a 20-minute bulk fermentation, then sheeted and chilled in a fridge or ice blankets for 30 min at 3-4°C. The dough is then processed using the **3-4-3** sequence resting in between every two folds in the freezer or ice blankets. When the pastry is made, it should again be rested for 30 minutes before sheeting in a freezer or ice blankets.

The pastry is then sheeted, cut, shaped, and placed in the proofer to ¾ proof stage at a temperature of 26-27°C and a relative humidity (RH) of 75-80%. So, for example, if the normal proof time for your croissant is 120 min, for pre proofed, the time needs to be reduced to 90 minutes. The pastry should be egg washed and blast frozen for 30 minutes at a temperature of -18°C to -20°C. Following the freezing process, the raw frozen croissants should be placed into a cardboard box with a plastic liner and sealed to prevent freezer burn. The frozen pre-proofed croissants should be stored at -18°C until required. To bake the frozen pre-proofed croissants off, the pastry should be removed from the cardboard storage box in the freezer. The pastries are then placed on baking trays and allowed to stand at room temperature for 10-15 minutes and then baked off at 170-180°C in a fan oven or 200°C in a deck oven for approximately 20 minutes.

Pre Proofed Frozen Croissant

Ingredients	1 Mix	1/2 Mix	Based on flour 100%	
			Bakers %	Hydration %
	Kg / g	Kg / g	1000	50.00
Overnight dough Stage 1				
Strong flour	1,000	500	100.0 %	
Water	500	250	50.0 %	
Sugar	100	50	10.0 %	
Fresh yeast	50	25	5.0 %	
Fresh sourdough starter 50/50	200	100	20.0 %	
Improver	10	5	1.0 %	
Salt	18	9	1.8 %	
Milk powder	40	20	4.0 %	
Butter	50	25	5.0 %	
Dough head weight	1,968	984	Butter on Dough %	Total Butter % in both Dough & Lamination
Lamination dough Stage 2				
Laminating butter	500	250	25.4	30.4
Total batch weight	2,468	1,234		
Yield	33	16		
Scaling wt in grams	75			

Figure 60: Pre-proofed frozen croissant recipe

Making croissants and viennoiserie using sourdough

Figure 61: Sourdough croissant 5-4-3 system

It is possible to make croissant and viennoiserie using only natural sourdough, using dosage levels of up to 28% of total flour weight and eliminating the yeast from the mix. The recipe below will produce excellent croissants when using the overnight fermentation method detailed earlier in the book, but this process will take three days as the pastry is made as follows:

Day1: Feed the starter, leave for 6 hrs, then make the dough. Ferment for 2-3 hrs, chill overnight @3°C

Day2: Make butter block, do a lock in-**3** then laminate with a 4-fold, followed by a 3-fold. Rest in the fridge for 40 minutes. Make up and wrap in plastic 20-22°C for 5-6 hrs, then place in the fridge overnight @3°C.

Day 3: Remove from fridge, egg wash and stand for 40min to 1 hour. Bake in a fan oven @175°C-180°C or a deck oven @200°C. Final proof could take an additional 5-7 hours, not a product for the faint-hearted due to the three days required to produce them.

Notes on sourdough croissant production

The sourdough should be very active and refreshed at least twice for three and a half hours between feeds and allowed to expand 2.5 to 3 times its mixed size for three hours at a time before mixing it into the croissant dough. The target pH of the sourdough should be 4.1 when adding to the croissant dough. The sourdough should not be too acidic as it will cause the dough to collapse during extended fermentation. The dough should be mixed in the usual manner specified earlier, without the addition of commercial yeast and allowed to ferment for 2-3 hours at 20-22°C then overnight in a fridge@3-4°C. The dough can then be processed as normal but may take up to three times longer to get some proof going (5-6 hrs+).

100% Sourdough Croissant

Ingredients	1 MIX	1/2 mix	Based on flour 100% Bakers %	Hydration %
	Kg / g	Kg / g	1000	49.60
Overnight dough Stage 1				
Strong Flour	1,000	500	100.0 %	
Milk	320	160	32.0 %	
Water	176	88	17.6 %	
Sugar	126	63	12.6 %	
Fresh sourdough starter 50/50	286	143	28.6 %	
Malt liquid	2	1	0.2 %	
Salt	16	8	1.6 %	
Butter	50	25	5.0 %	
Dough head weight	1,976	988	Butter on Dough %	Total Butter % in both Dough & Lamination
Lamination dough Stage 2				
Laminating butter	550	275	27.8	32.8
Total batch weight	2,526	1,263		
Yield	34	17		
Scaling wt in grams	75			

Sweet puff paste 3-4-4 / 4

Stages of production:

First **3** lock-in   The first stage of the process-3 layers

Second 4-fold   3 x 4 layers   =   12 layers-3 where dough touches dough = 9 layers

Third 4-fold   9 x 4 layers   =   36 layers-3 where dough touches dough = 33 layers

Resting phase   Wrap in plastic, place in the fridge @3°C for 30-40 minutes

Fourth 4-fold   33 x 4 layers   =   132 layers-3 where dough touches dough = 129 layers

Puff paste is not as time-consuming as it is made out to be and when made with butter, is a delightful product which has many amazing possibilities. Using the folding numeric sequences detailed earlier, puff paste may be produced both swiftly and efficiently. The dough should ideally be mixed the day before and stored overnight in a fridge at 3-4°C. The dough is then removed from the fridge and the butter block placed over the centre of the dough. The pastry is then folded into a **3** for the lock-in. The dough is then sheeted, and a 4-fold is given to the dough. The dough is then given another 4-fold and at this stage, the block of pastry should be placed in the freezer wrapped in plastic for a half-hour or placed between two ice blankets for 20 minutes. The butter puff paste is now at the halfway stage.

After resting in the freezer, the pastry can be sheeted once more and given its final 4-fold. The pastry should then be placed in the freezer or between ice blankets for a further 45 minutes and can be processed or frozen. If the pastry is to be processed at this stage, after sheeting and cutting, the pastry should be allowed to rest for one hour before baking to prevent shrinkage or overnight in a fridge.

Sweet Puff Paste Dough

Ingredients	1 Mix	1/2 Mix	Based on flour 100%	
			Bakers %	Hydration %
	Kg / g	Kg / g	1000	53.00
Overnight dough Stage 1				
Strong flour	1,000	500	100.0 %	
Water	460	230	46.0 %	
Egg	70	35	7.0 %	
Sugar	20	10	2.0 %	
Butter unsalted	60	30	6.0 %	
Salt	20	10	2.0 %	
Dough head weight	1,630	815	**Butter on**	Total Butter %
			Dough %	in both
Lamination dough Stage 2				Dough & Lamination
Laminating butter	1,000	500	61.3	67.3
Total batch weight	2,630	1,315		
Yield	35	18		
Scaling wt in grams	75			

Figure 62: Sweet puff paste recipe

Palmiers are a personal favourite, and if palmiers are being made from butter puff pastry, copious quantities of sugar should be applied following sheeting of the third 4-fold. The sugar should also be gently squeezed into the pastry at this stage using light pressure from a rolling pin or on a sheeter.

Figure 63: Butter palmier and butterfly palmier

The pastry with the butter and sugar should be handled carefully and sheeted out to a thickness of 3-4cm. More sugar is applied over all the pastry and gently rolled into the pastry using a rolling pin, before shaping into palmiers. The palmiers should be cut and placed on trays allowing ample room for the pastry to expand during baking. The palmiers are baked in a rack or oven at a temperature of 190°C for 20 minutes. Following baking, the pastry should be allowed to cool on the tray and removed to a wire rack to prevent the pastry from becoming soggy. They can be sold individually, sandwiched with cream or sealed into plastic bags to prevent them from absorbing moisture from the air. Many savoury products can also be made from puff paste. The recipe below has no sugar and can be used as a base for many savoury items such as sausage rolls, veggie rolls, cheese twists to name but a few.

Figure 64: Apple pie with butter puff paste

Savoury puff paste recipe 3-4-4 / 4

I have included a savoury recipe for puff paste, this recipe makes good pastry for savoury products including sausage rolls. I have included it as a cheaper option to the extra flaky pastry on the next page, which is a premium and expensive pastry due to large quantities of butter and egg in the recipe. The hydration comparison is interesting when compared to the extra flaky puff paste. The larger quantity of butter in the dough of the extra flaky recipe lowers the hydration, making the pastry very crispy indeed.

Savoury Puff Paste

Ingredients	1 MIX	1/2 mix	Based on flour 100%	
			Bakers %	Hydration %
	Kg / g	Kg / g	1000	60.30
Overnight dough Stage 1				
Bread flour	1,000	500	100.0 %	
Egg	455	228	45.5 %	
Water	148	74	14.8 %	
Butter unsalted	60	30	6.0 %	
Salt	20	10	2.0 %	
Dough head weight	1,683	842	**Butter on**	Total Butter %
			Dough %	in both
Lamination dough Stage 2				Dough & Lamination
Laminating butter	1,000	500	59.4	65.4
Total batch weight	2,683	1,342		
Yield	36	18		
Scaling wt in grams	75			

Extra flaky puff paste 3-3-3 / 3-3

I make a beautiful quiche filling with 250g double cream, 250g milk, 175g egg, 10g salt and 2g pepper. This base is rich and creamy, and both vegetarian and meat accompaniments are fantastic when used with this pastry recipe. It melts in your mouth, leaving you seeking another as the rich flavour stays on your palate too long! Patience is key with this pastry, the dough is made day one and lamination, and bake is made the following day. The pastry is very flaky, a joy to eat. The filling for cheese and onion quiche is white onion 300g red onion 300g, butter 50g, balsamic vinegar 50g, salt 2.5g, black pepper 1.5g fry together and reduce on a frying pan. Allow to cool. Line a 32cm quiche dish with puff paste. Add the cooled, fried onion mix. Pour the quiche base mix into the quiche dish, fill to 4/5ths. Sprinkle 60g of grated Gruyere cheese on the top and bake for 45-50 minutes @180°C. You can use also broccoli/courgettes/mushrooms/tomato/bacon/ham or any other fillings you like in the quiche

Puff paste quiche with cheese and onion

Extra Flaky Puff Paste

Ingredients	1 Mix	1/2 Mix	Based on flour 100%	
			Bakers %	Hydration %
	Kg / g	Kg / g	1000	35.30
Overnight dough Stage 1				
Soft biscuit flour	1,000	500	100.0 %	
Egg	205	103	20.5 %	
Water	148	74	14.8 %	
Sugar	68	34	6.8 %	
Butter unsalted	375	188	37.5 %	
Salt	14	7	1.4 %	
Dough head weight	1,810	905	**Butter on Dough %**	Total Butter % in both Dough & Lamination
Lamination dough Stage 2				
Laminating butter	500	250	27.6	65.1
Total batch weight	2,310	1,155		
Yield	31	15		
Scaling wt in grams	75			

Mix all ingredients in a bowl, ensuring that the butter in the dough is at room temperature and using the hook attachment; mix Stage 1 on a dough mixer for 4 minutes on slow speed and three minutes on second speed. Pinout to 12mm, cover with plastic and store in the fridge covered for at least 30 minutes or overnight. Prepare the butter block in a rectangular shape as demonstrated before and store in the fridge until the dough is ready to laminate. Lamination is split into two resting stages indicated after the third 3-fold in the sequence by a separator or /.

The rolling sequence for this type of puff paste is a **3-3-3 / 3-3-** sequence.

First 3-fold the lock-in - **3** layers

Second 3-fold 3 x 3 layers = 9 layers – 2 points where dough touches dough layers   =   7

Third 3-fold 7 x 3 layers = 21 layers – 2 points where dough touches dough layers   =   19

NB: It is important to rest the dough for at least a half an hour in a fridge before giving it the remaining two folds.

Fourth 3-fold 19 x 3 layers = 57 layers – 2 points where dough touches dough   =55 layers.

Fifth 3-fold 55 x 3 layers = 165 layers - 2 points where dough touches dough   =163 layers.

Chill in the fridge for 45-60 minutes and sheet to make quiche, sausage roll and a range of assorted goods.

Puff paste is not as time-consuming as it is made out to be and when made with butter, is a delightful product which has many amazing possibilities. Using the folding numeric sequences detailed earlier, puff paste may be produced both swiftly and efficiently.

The 3-4-4 / 4 system

The dough should ideally be mixed the day before and stored overnight in a fridge at 3-4°C. The dough is then removed from the fridge and the butter block placed over the centre of the dough and folded into a **3** for the lock-in. The dough is then sheeted to 4mm and a further 4-fold is given to the dough. The dough is then sheeted once more and given another 4-fold, and at this stage, the block of dough should be placed in the freezer wrapped in plastic for a half-hour or placed between two ice blankets for 20 minutes. The butter puff paste requires one last fold to complete the lamination sequence.

After resting in the freezer, the block of dough can be given a final 4-fold. The dough should then be placed in the freezer or between ice blankets for a further 20-30 minutes and can be processed or frozen. If the pastry is to be processed at this stage, after sheeting and cutting, the pastry should be allowed to rest for one hour before baking to prevent shrinkage.

Laminated brioche

Laminated brioche is a very highly enriched pastry which is made with a butter brioche dough plus the addition of 50.7% butter based on total dough weight. The pre-dough starter contains water, but the liquids in the main dough include milk, eggs, and egg yolks. The higher hydration laminated brioche pastries are popular throughout France and Europe and command a great price for the quality of ingredients and the process used. Laminated brioche can also be used to make the legendary "Cronut ™" style product, where the pastry is proofed and then float fried instead of baked. Laminated brioche can be sold in small or larger units, typically baked in a fluted brioche shape of which there are an infinite amount of sizes. Individual brioche are made in a similar manner to pain aux raisins, rolled into a sheet, then coiled up and cut into pieces. The smaller ones were 2 cm wide and weighed 60g, the larger ones were 600g and the shape I used was 25cm wide at the top. Brioche shapes can be purchased in metal and there are also one-use disposable cardboard ones coated with silicone. I used these disposable ones in the photos page 120.

Laminated Brioche

Ingredients	1 Mix	1/2 Mix	Based on flour 100%	
			Bakers %	Hydration %
	Kg / g	Kg / g	1420	65.63
Predough Stage 1				
Bakers flour	160	80	11.3 %	
Water	100	50	7.0 %	
Fresh yeast	3	2	0.2 %	
Salt	3	2	0.2 %	
	266	133		
Dough Stage 2				
Predough	266	133	18.7	
Strong flour	1,260	630	88.7 %	
Milk	192	96	13.5 %	
Egg yolk	80	40	5.6 %	
Whole egg	560	280	39.4 %	
Sugar	180	90	12.7 %	
Fresh yeast	63	32	4.4 %	
Malt liquid	25	13	1.8 %	
Salt	27	14	1.9 %	
Butter	227	114	16.0 %	

	1 Mix	1/2 Mix	Butter on Dough %	Total Butter % in both Dough & Lamination
Dough head weight	2,880	1,440		
Lamination Dough Stage 2				
Laminating butter	1,000	500	34.7	50.7

Total batch weight	3,880	1,940
Yield brioche 60g	65	32
Scaling wt in grams	60	
Yield brioche 600g	6	3
Scaling wt in grams	600	

Figure 65: Laminated brioche recipe, note the high butter content

Figure 66: Laminated brioche raw in a fluted shape

The laminated brioche dough should be kept chilled at all stages of the lamination process as outlined earlier in this book by keeping the enriched dough. The lamination sequence for the small pieces is **3**-4-3 or **5**-4-3 for larger pieces. Laminated brioche is typically sold plain, without filling and due to the high levels of enrichment, will keep well if packaged in a re-sealable plastic bag.

Figure 67: Laminated Brioche small pieces

Kouign Amann 3-4-4

Figure 68: Raspberry rhubarb Kouign amann

The Kouign-amann was first invented in 1860; a speciality pastry of the town of Douarnenez in Finistère, Brittany, France (Lonely Planet Food, 2017). The delicious creation is credited to Baker Yves-René Scordia (1828-1878). Kouign-amann is a traditional Breton cake. The name originates from the Breton language combining the words for cake (kouign) and butter (amann). Kouign-amann is a round crusty pastry, originally made from bread dough, but made today using a rich viennoiserie dough. The Kouign-amann is a form of laminated brioche with many layers of butter and sugar folded in, similar in manner to puff pastry although with less laminated layers. Salted butter is used both in the pastry and to grease the 7cm wide x 4cm high metal rings used to bake the Kouign-amann. The pastry is a three-day process. Day 1, the pre dough is made and fermented @19°C overnight. Day 2, the dough is mixed in two stages, 4 minutes on slow, 5 minutes on 2nd speed, ensuring that the dough is well developed before adding the butter and mixing to clear for a further 3-4 minutes. The DDT is 26°C and the dough should be fermented for 45 minutes at room temperature, then placed in the fridge at 3°C overnight. The pastry is made using the **3-4-4** laminating system, but copious amounts of sugar are added to the sheeted pastry before the final 4-fold. The pastry is sheeted to 4mm, cut into 10cm squares, roughly 75g each. The four corners are then folded to the centre and the pastry is placed in the steel rings. The pastry is proofed at a low temperature 25-26°C and low humidity to ensure that the salted butter layers and the sugar do not melt before baking. Toppings applied before baking included crème pâtissière, apple, Nutella, raspberry/rhubarb and chopped raspberry pear marinade on page 132.They are slowly baked at 190ºC for 20-25 minutes until the pastry achieves maximum oven spring and the sugar caramelises. The baked pastry resembles a laminated muffin-shape and is essentially a salted caramelised croissant in a round shape. Kerrygold Irish butter is used in this recipe for its quality and flavour.

Figure 69: The buttered-sugared shapes for Kouign amann

Kougin-amann

Ingredients	1 Mix	1/2 Mix	Bakers %	Hydration %
	Kg / g	Kg / g	665	66.02
Predough stage 1				
Bakers flour	35	18	5.3 %	
Water	23	12	3.5 %	
Fresh yeast	0.6	0.3	0.1 %	
Salt	1	0.3	0.1 %	
	59	30		
Dough stage 2				
Predough	133	133	20.0	
Strong flour	630	315	94.7 %	
Milk	96	48	14.4 %	
Egg yolk	40	20	6.0 %	
Whole egg	280	140	42.1 %	
Sugar	90	45	13.5 %	
Fresh yeast	32	16	4.8 %	
Malt liquid	13	7	2.0 %	
Salt	12	6	1.8 %	
Butter addition stage 3				
Butter	114	57	17.1 %	
Dough head weight	1,440	787	**Butter on Dough %**	Total butter % in both Dough & Lamination
Lamination stage 4				
Kerrygold salted butter	500	250	34.7	**51.9**
Total batch weight	1,940	1,037		
Yield 75g	26	14		
Scaling wt in grams	75			

Figure 70: Kouign amann recipe

Coupe du Monde Chocolatine, Toulouse, France. 2019

An invitation came from Toulouse, France, to participate in the Coupe du Monde Chocolatine (CDMC) or the World Cup Chocolatine Championships from the organiser Geraldine Laborde. I accepted the invitation and the challenge of the competition and used the invitation as a great reason to motivate me into top-level competition mode once more. I had not competed in over 25 years but decided to rise to the challenge and practised daily from April until the end of May. I travelled to Toulouse and enjoyed the company of Geraldine and her little dog Marvel. She brought me to the old city where she went to the hairdressers, and I went off with her dog to do some sightseeing. Toulouse is a beautiful old city with a massive square which houses the Townhall and many architecturally historic and important buildings. There is much to see and do in Toulouse, beautiful open-air spaces where one can dine alfresco, and people watch as well as century-old churches and a great choice of shops. We met up with some friends of Geraldine and later went for a meal and to a Scottish bar for a drink.

Geraldine took me to the centre of Toulouse, where the yellow jacket protesters were in full swing. Robocop type police wearing full riot gear in their hundreds were also present, and the vans which had transported them to the city were parked as far as the eye could see. It was a surreal experience, I kept away from all the skirmishes which were breaking out between police and protesters and took refuge with Geraldine in the first floor of an Irish Pub as water cannons and tear gas began to be used by the police. I witnessed many baton charges and could smell the sickly tear gas as it permeated the building. Outside was a warzone, and I wondered how long it would take to be safe to leave. Two hours later, after a light lunch, the crowds had dispersed, and we walked through the city. All the banks and multinational companies such as Burger King, McDonald's and many others were closed and boarded up with wood. It was sad to see this, but the French have even back to revolution days been very vociferous about political matters and are prepared to fight for what they think is right. The following morning, I went back to a local baker called David, who opened his production facility to some of the competitors. We prepared our doughs and ingredients for the world championship the day before the competition. It was at David's bakery I met with fellow competitor Christophe Secondi from Corsica, and we hit it off as buddies straight away. Christophe would travel to Galway later in the year to visit me with his family. Having completed preparations for the event, all candidates were invited on a walking tour of Toulouse, and we even got to sample a special local delicacy of chocolatine ice cream. We all had dinner al fresco in a square off the main thoroughfare and got to chat and meet with members of the jury and other competitors. I returned early to the hotel to get a good night's sleep and prepare for competition, the world championships beckoned, and I wanted to be on top of my game on the day. The Coupe du Monde Chocolatine was a true artisan competition. It tested one's manual skills and abilities to the limit. Apart from mixing and ingredient preparation, all lamination, butter preparation, cutting and shaping had to be done by hand with a rolling pin, and mechanical lamination machines were not allowed. Very stringent rules regarding the quantity of dough and the baked weight of the pieces were strictly enforced as well as each candidate being assigned a supervisor to ensure that all work was following the rules and to a very high level of hygiene and professionalism. Over 40 bakers from several nations competed on the day in two shifts as there was limited equipment and space for all to work at the same time. I had rehearsed the production of my pastries many times and launched into my 4 allocated hours of production time. I finished with 10 minutes to spare and was very pleased with my results. I would miss the tasting and marking by the 48-jury member panel and the prize-giving ceremony as I had to fly to the UK for some classes. I left for the airport in Toulouse and took my first leg flight which touched down in Brussels airport and decided to get a bite to eat. As I was eating my pasta in the restaurant, my phone rang, and it was Geraldine Laborde who called to inform me of my silver medal placing in the world championships, I was over the moon with excitement and did not expect a podium finish. I was absolutely delighted with my result and felt joy, privilege and success had come my way. Now I will share my recipe with you.

Figure 71: World Silver Medal, Coupe Du Monde Chocolatine

World Silver Medal 2019 Coupe du Monde Chocolatine 3-4-4

Description

The Chocolatine Classique is a masterpiece of French ingenuity and creativity. Also incorrectly known as Pain au Chocolat globally and in France, this viennoiserie identity is on a par with the croissant worldwide as an iconic French classic. It is enjoyed not only as a breakfast pastry but at any time of the day as a sweet treat by millions of people daily. This recipe makes two dough heads at 700g add 200g butter for lamination of each dough head. This recipe gives 2 x 12 pieces. I use the same base recipe for both doughs.

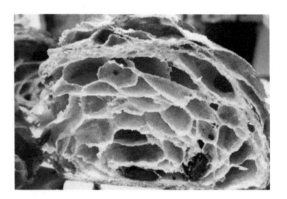

Ingredients/recipe for 2 x 700g	Quantity	%	Production method 3-4-4 Lamination system
Gruau Flour T-45	365	45.6	Mix for 8 min 1st speed, and 5 min 2nd speed on a planetary mixer with a dough hook
Tradition flour T-55	365	45.6	Desired dough temperature 24°C
Water	300	37.5	Scale into 1 x 700g head of dough
Liquid Levain	140	17.5	Place in a container overnight, covered with plastic
Sugar	104	13	and leave in a fridge at 2°C, Laminate 3-4-4
Yeast (Fresh)	32	4	Cool down again for 45 min at 2°C, thin out @ 25min
Malt (Liquid)	2	0.3	Roll to 3mm and cut rectangle of 14mm L x 8 mm W
Salt	14	1.8	Shape the Chocolatines , use two bars of 6g each
Butter	80	10	Weight should be 68-71g before baking.
Pate fermentee	4	0.5	Final proof time 2 - 2.5 hours at 27°C
Use 700g dough to 200g butter			Egg wash the Chocolatine, rest 10 minutes on the table
Lamination butter% dough wt	2 x 200	28.4	Bake in a convection oven @ 170° 17 -18 min

Physical and flavour characteristics

An external aspect includes the light crispy crumb combined with the natural brilliance of the egg wash on the hand-laminated butter pastry. The addition of malt to the dough accelerates the Maillard reaction during baking, giving a pleasing chestnut colour to the exterior crust and enhancing flavour. Finally, a layer of chocolate croissant dough highlights the flavour, colour and lamination in the inside honeycomb texture. The baked chocolatine is allowed to cool and is then carefully stencilled using a small sprinkle of icing sugar with a 4-leaf clover design for greater eye appeal.

Description

The Orange chocolate praline twist is a variation of the original, but out of respect to the original, all of the elements of making this classic are retained, while other features are added. A thin sheet of chocolate dough is placed on the laminated dough just before sheeting, and when cut into rectangles, the dough then is cut into 5 even pieces. The middle three are twisted twice, giving this Innovative chocolatine a special twist, extra crispiness and texture are added from the light dusting of cocoa, icing sugar and orange bubble sugar after baking. This recipe makes 2 dough heads at 700g add 200g butter for lamination of each dough head. This recipe gives 2 x 12 pieces. I use the same base recipe for both doughs. Special instructions for the chocolate dough are on the next page.

 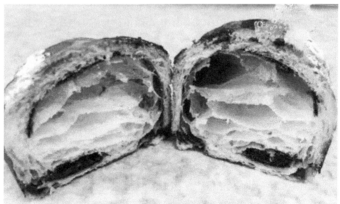

Ingredients/recipe 2 x 700g	Quantity	%	Production method 3-4-4 Lamination system
Gruau Flour T-45	365	45.6	Mix for 8 min 1st speed, and 5 min 2nd speed on a planetary mixer with a dough hook.
Tradition flour T-55	365	45.6	Desired dough temperature 24°C
Water	300	37.5	Scale 1 x 700g head of dough, make 157g choc dough
Liquid Levain	140	17.5	Place in a container overnight, covered with plastic
Sugar	104	13	and leave in a fridge at 2°C Laminate 3-4-4
Yeast (Fresh)	32	4	Cool down again for 45 min at 2°C, thin out @ 25min
Malt (Liquid)	2	0.3	Roll to 3mm and cut rectangle of 14mm L x 8 mm W
Salt	14	1.8	Cut into 5, twist the middle 3 strands, roll up
Butter	80	10	Use 1 bar of 12g each piece should be -78-88g
Pate fermentee	4	0.5	Final proof time 2 hours at 27°C
Use 700g dough to 200g butter			Egg wash the Chocolatine, rest 10 minutes on the table
Lamination butter% dough wt	2 x 200	28.4	Bake in a convection oven @ 170°C for 20– 22 minutes

Physical and flavour characteristics

Moulds were specially created to enable this chocolatine to keep its shape. External aspects include the three twists of this bicolour dough in the centre and the careful dusting after baking of dark Dutch cocoa, icing sugar, homemade candied orange and bubble sugar which mirrors the light internal texture. Finally, a layer of chocolate croissant dough highlights the flavour, colour and lamination aspect on the internal texture.

The added value of the product

The innovative chocolatine can cool and is then carefully stencilled, with icing sugar on one side and cocoa on the other. Candied peel is added to the centre along with a touch of orange bubble sugar to give this chocolatine a unique finish and beautiful textures in the mouth on the pallet.

Description

After 8 minutes mixing the dough recipe on 1st speed, I remove a piece of dough from the mix weighing 120g. I prepare 12g cocoa powder, 10g butter, 5g of water and 10g fresh yeast, and when the main dough is mixed, I put the 120g of dough into the bowl with the cocoa mix and mix together for 5 minutes on 2nd speed to get a nice chocolate dough mix which I will use to top the pastry once it is laminated. I carefully scale the white dough with the chocolate dough to ensure I have just the 700g required for the competition. The small remaining piece, 37g of white dough, is kept as a pâté fermentée for use in the next dough, so there is no wastage.

Shaping the innovative chocolatine

The chocolatine pastry is rolled to 3.5mm with the chocolate side down and then cut into 12 pieces of approximately 14mm x 8mm; each is then divided into five. The central three strands are twisted three times. The homemade chocolate bar is added. The chocolatine is then rolled up and placed in a special metal form to prevent the sides from falling over, and to retain the chocolatine shape/aspect.

Ingredients / recipe for bar	Quantity	%	Production method
Chocolate Noir	120g		Melt the chocolate
Praline Hazelnut paste	40g		Add the orange oil
Roasted nib hazelnut	100g		Add the praline
Orange Oil	2g		Finally blend the crushed hazelnuts
			Pipe into 12g bars and cool in freezer
Yield 21 bars @ 12g each			
Bubble Sugar Recipe			**Method:**
			Blitz Isomalt sticks and colour on a blender
Isomalt	100g		Add a drop of Orange oil
Orange powder colour	1g		Place a teaspoon full of mixture into 2cm steel rings
Orange Oil	1g		on a silicone mat
			Place in oven 185°C Melt 7-10 Min
			Allow to cool and break off pieces as required

The special shape for the "Innovative Chocolatine" challenge

Description:

Especially for this competition, I got 12 x 2mm thick stainless-steel shapes made. The moulds are 80mm wide, 80mm long and 75mm deep on the outside. Proofing and baking in these moulds prevent the ends from falling over and distorting the shape. The result is a distinctly similar shape to the original chocolatine, but with a twist.

I wanted to create a new chocolatine which keeps all the aspects of the chocolatine we all know and love but set this one apart, as being an innovative luxury version of the original classic, with a homemade crunchy praline orange bar. Colour, aspect, appearance and texture were given a lot of thought to reflect the flavours of orange, chocolate and hazelnut in this innovative chocolatine creation.

While innovative by nature, the shape and textures of this chocolatine are true to the original creation. The orange bubble sugar reflecting the flavours and honeycomb internal structure.

Raspberry pear marinade 3-4-3

The raspberry pear marinade has become one of my most recognisable pastries and a signature dish. The marinade is best made a few days before using the pears as the colour and flavours increase with age. You will need two small tins of pear halves, there are usually 6 pear halves per small tin. You will also need 60g sugar, 50g frozen raspberries, 5g raspberry alcohol and some vanilla to taste. The mixture is boiled and simmered for 5 minutes. The marinade for 12 pastries is made by the following method: The juice from the tinned pears is strained into a saucepan. The sugar and raspberry purée are added to the pear juice, the vanilla is added, and the mixture is brought to the boil and allowed to simmer for 5 minutes. The syrup should be set aside to cool, at which point the Raspberry alcohol is added, and finally the pears. The pink syrup mixture with the pears should be placed in a sealed container, covered and put in the fridge at 3°C for two days to ensure correct colouration of the pears. You will need to make crème patisserie to pipe and freeze as 5cm mini eclairs in advance. I have made a YouTube video on how to pipe the frozen crème pâtissière bars, see link for making frozen Créme Pâtisserie pieces for viennoiserie https://youtu.be/kwUZEcjtak4 on my YouTube channel.

The Crème Pâtissière recipe

Stage1: Mix together to form a paste

125g	Milk	Whisk and boil together, prepare stage 2
25g	Sugar	

Stage 2:   Whisk all stage 2 together and add to stage 1

25g	Caster sugar
33g	Flour soft wheat
50g	Egg yolks (2 approx.)
125g	Milk

Vanilla pod scraped (1g) to extract the seeds or use vanilla essence

Stage 3:   Remove stages 1&2 from the heat and add the butter, whisk to clear.

30g	Butter
414g	**Total weight**

Method detail:

Heat the stage 1 milk and half of the sugar to boiling point in a small saucepan. Weigh the rest of the stage 2 ingredients separately and whisk with a hand whisk to a fluffy and smooth mixture. Once the stage 1 milk/sugar boils, remove from the heat and pour the mixture from stage 2 into the saucepan and whisk gently. Put the pan on the heat again and keep stirring with the hand whisk until the mix thickens (generally the cooking time is 2/3 minutes per kilo of milk).Once cooked, take it off the heat and add the butter to it, keep stirring until it is fully absorbed then spread the crème pâtissière onto a clean tray lined with clingfilm, then dust with icing sugar to prevent a skin forming. Cover and place the crème pâtissière in the fridge to cool. Store in a refrigerator when cool, beat the crème pâtissière on a stand mixer with a cake beater to soften it to piping consistency and pipe into fingers as previously described and freeze.

Preparation and cutting of the pastry

For the raspberry pear viennoiserie, the pastry is sheeted to a thickness of 7mm and chilled again for 20 minutes to stiffen the butter and the pastry dough to enable cutting, without shrinking the pastry. Using a large pear-shaped or teardrop-shaped cutter 16cm long x10cm wide, cut the bases and place on a tray. The pear-shaped pastry pieces are placed on a tray with silicone paper, egg-washed and proofed at a temperature of 27°C for 60-90 minutes at 75-80% relative humidity. The temperature is critical as, if it exceeds 28°C, the butter will liquefy and run out of the dough, destroying the lamination layers.

When proofed, the frozen custard fingers are placed in the centre of the proofed pastry and given a gentle shove downwards to embed them into the pastry. The function of the frozen custard fingers is to prevent the custard from leaking out over the edges as the pastry rises. Check out my YouTube channel below to see how the technique is done.

How to insert frozen Créme Pâtisserie into proofed pastry https://youtu.be/NBm1Ti-YAWU

Raspberry Jam is then piped onto the frozen custard and, finally, the rinsed, dried raspberry pears are sliced 5 times from right to left but leaving the upper part of the pear attached. The sliced raspberry pear is placed on the custard and pressed down to prevent it from falling over in the oven while baking.

Using a ventilated, or fan oven, pre-set the temperature at 230°C, load the pastry and close the oven door. Reset the temperature to 175°C and bake for 22-24 minutes. The baked pastry should be allowed to cool, then glazed with nappage or apricot jam. Using a bench scraper, with the blade placed 3mm from the edge of each pastry at a 45° angle, the pastries are dusted with icing sugar. The same is done at the slender tip side of each pastry using a dusting of raspberry powder. Finally, a fresh raspberry is placed at the top of the baked pear on the pastry. If required, red chocolate hearts may also be sprinkled on the baked pear to finalise the garnish.

Chocolate pear baskets 3-4-3

Using the same teardrop-shaped cutter as above for the raspberry pear marinade, this creation is a delicate chocolate pear basket. The thin end of the tear is rolled out thinly, frozen créme pâtisserie is placed on top the pastry, followed by 2 chocolate bars, and half a small pear half. The tip is stretched over the pear and tucked in under the pastry gently. As the pastry proofs, the tip gently releases from under the proofing pastry, and a handle appears to form on this beautifully tasty pastry. Can be made with chocolate….

Or without! Simply insert a disc of frozen crème pâtissière into the teardrop-shaped piece of pastry, add a half of a poached/tin pear, proof and bake. Add some raspberry jam on the inside, and after baking, a sprinkle of raspberry powder to garnish.

Pain aux raisins 3-4-3

Using the pastry recipe page 139; a ½ mix will make approximately 16-18 units. Use the crème pâtissière recipe on page 132. Golden raisins are wonderful in this product and should be washed the day before use. Additionally, they can be soaked with a little rum for added flavour. Weigh all your ingredients and place them into the mixing bowl (except the lamination butter). Shape your butter into a rectangle butter block and place in the fridge. Using the dough hook with an electric mixer, mix on slow speed for about 4 minutes or until the dough combines then mix on second speed until smooth (roughly 4 minutes). Roll the dough into a rectangular shape, place into a plastic bag on a baking tray then place in the fridge overnight. Remove the croissant dough out of the fridge, roll it out in a rectangle until it is twice the size of the butter. Make a Lock-in **3**. Slice the closed dough edge (sandwich method) to release the elastic recoil. Rotate the dough 90° then sheet to 3mm and make a 4-fold (approximately 4 times longer than when you first placed the butter in). Place the pastry back in the fridge to rest until it is cold (20-30 minutes). Cut the closed edges to ease the elastic recoil and sheet to 4mm; make a 3-fold, rest in the fridge up to 60 minutes @3°C. Sheeting stage: Sheet the dough to between 5/6mm thick to a rectangle (45cm width). Spread crème pâtissière evenly, leaving a good 2cm strip of the pastry free from crème pâtissière at the base, sprinkle raisins all over then start rolling firmly like a swiss roll, but not too tight from top to base. Roll towards yourself, it is easier! Mark and cut the roll to into slices (2/3cm thick) using a very sharp serrated tooth knife. Tuck the ends in to prevent them from opening up in the proof stage, then place them on baking trays using baking paper and place in the proofer. Proof time can vary and can take up to 2.5 hours at 26°C with 75% relative humidity. Remove trays from the proofer, egg wash gently all over. Place trays in a pre-heated oven (210°C for a deck oven, 180°C for a fan oven) until you get a lovely golden-brown crust. Bake for approximately 15 minutes depending on product size to a golden-brown colour. When cool, brush with boiled apricot jam to finish; then drizzle with warm fondant or water icing, you can also garnish with a half glacé cherry.

Pain Aux Raisins

Ingredients	1 Mix	1/2 Mix	Based on flour 100% Bakers %	Hydration %
	Kg / g	Kg / g	1000	48.50
Overnight dough Stage 1				
Strong flour	1,000	500	100.0 %	
Water	485	243	48.5 %	
Sugar	120	60	12.0 %	
Fresh yeast	40	20	4.0 %	
Salt	18	9	1.8 %	
Milk powder	30	15	3.0 %	
Dough head weight	1,693	847	**Butter on Dough %**	Total butter % in both
Lamination dough Stage 2				Dough & Lamination
Laminating butter	550	275	32.5	32.5
Total batch weight	2,243	1,122		
Yield	32	16		
Scaling wt in grams	70			
Additions to the pastry:				
Crème pâtissière	1000g	500g		
Raisins	600g	300g		

Cinnamon swirls 3-4-3

Cinnamon swirls are a delicious alternative for those who do not like raisins or other dried fruits. They are made up exactly the same way as pain aux raisins. Use the recipe on page 141 for the pastry. The crème pâtissière (page 132) is mixed with cinnamon sugar, to make cinnamon custard. The cinnamon custard is spread on the pastry allowing a good 2cm of the pastry free of cinnamon custard at the base, so it can be sealed. Moisten this piece of the pastry by brushing with a damp pastry brush; then start rolling the pastry towards you like a Swiss roll (not too tight) from top to base. Cut the roll to slices (2/3cm thick) then place on baking trays using baking paper and place in the proofer. Proof and bake the same as the pain aux raisins in the previous recipe. For extra crunchiness, nibbed or crushed sugar can be added just before baking.

Cinnamon Swirls

Ingredients	1 Mix	1/2 Mix	Based on flour 100%	
			Bakers %	**Hydration %**
	Kg / g	Kg / g	1000	48.50
Overnight dough Stage 1				
Strong flour	1,000	500	100.0 %	
Water	485	243	48.5 %	
Sugar	120	60	12.0 %	
Fresh yeast	40	20	4.0 %	
Salt	18	9	1.8 %	
Milk powder	30	15	3.0 %	
Dough head weight	1,693	847	**Butter on Dough %**	**Total Butter % in both Dough & Lamination**
Lamination dough Stage 2				
Laminating butter	550	275	32.5	32.5
Total batch weight	2,243	1,122		
Yield	32	16		
Scaling wt in grams	70			
Additions to the pastry:				
Cinnamon	40	20		
Brown sugar	160	80		
Crème pâtissière	1000	500		

Beautiful cinnamon custard at the heart of these delicious cinnamon swirls, sprinkled with crushed sugar just before baking, otherwise the sugar will dissolve on the egg wash and turn to syrup.

Other ideas to stimulate the mind

Apple Pistachio/Apple Raspberry

 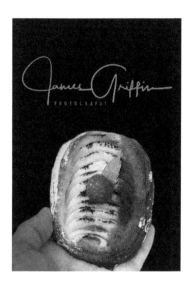

Apple-Pistachio with crème pâtissière 3-4-3. These lovely pastries are cut from pastry sheeted to 5mm thick using a Matfer brand oval-shaped-cutter. The oval cutter measurements I use are 12.5cm long x 9cm wide. The pastries are proofed without any toppings to full volume. Flat cut pastries like this take less time to proof as there is only one layer of pastry, which is not coiled like a croissant and as a result, the core temperature rises quickly. They generally take 60-90 minutes to proof. Once proofed, they should be egg washed, and frozen crème pâtissière (page 132) bars should be placed inverted (top of frozen crème pâtissière) on the proofed dough and pressed into the pastry, so the flat base of the frozen custard is facing up. This flat surface is perfect for placing your sliced apples on. Use small apples when preparing the pastries, and I use half an apple sliced thinly on each pastry. Fan the apples out evenly and press fully down. The apple slices will stick to the egg wash and remain in place for the bake. Bake for 25 min 180-195°C. The apple topping takes longer to bake than a plain croissant. Once baked and cooled, the pastries are glazed with apricot nappage and garnished with freshly ground pistachio nut to finish. A raspberry variety can also be made by adding raspberry jam under the apple before baking and dusting one side with raspberry powder, the other with icing sugar after baking, cooling and glazing with apricot jam.

Cappuccino Chocolatine three types of pastry

Cappuccino Cream Chocolatine - Made with three types of pastry combined, cappuccino coffee, chocolate and vanilla pastry. Each pastry has three types of butter, chocolate butter, instant coffee butter and a plain variety, add vanilla to the dough for extra flavour. Lamination sequence for each dough is **3**-4 (9 layers) stack on top of each other (3 x 9=27)-2 DTP, total layers 25, same as croissant **3**-4-3. Sheet out, cut, proof and bake. Finish as above or use your imagination for a personalised finish.

Raspberry/Strawberry Chocolatine

Made using 10% raspberry or strawberry powder in the butter, this chocolatine also has raspberry jam as a filling and was made using my croissant recipe on page 51. Cut, shape, proof and bake as per chocolatine.

Strawberry Shortcake

Vanilla streusel recipe- use pastry flour	
Stage 1	
Butter 100g	Cream the butter and sugar together
Sugar 100g	
Vanilla 2g	or use vanilla essence
Stage 2	
Flour 125g	Add to above and mix to a paste
Freeze until required. Alternatively mix to a crumb and refrigerate until required	
Triangle steel shapes 10cm length x 4.5cm high	

This triangle-shaped viennoiserie has laminated pastry base, chocolate brioche middle layer, strawberry puree/jam and topped with vanilla streusel, then sprinkled with icing sugar and pistachio post bake. The base was cut out of croissant dough 4mm thick, the brioche was cut out 3mm thick and the strawberry puree piped on the brioche. They are proofed for 90 minutes in The streusel is applied just before baking

Nutella/Coffee

Made using 10% instant coffee in the butter and the pastry recipe on page 51, this chocolatine had Nutella piped inside after baking, a swirl of butter cream, chocolate flake and hazelnut to decorate. Cut and shape as per chocolatine.

Raspberry Brioche Sablée

Possibly one of my favourite viennoiseries, and taught to me by my dear friend François Wolfisberg, who is located in Carouge, Switzerland. François and I met in the late 1990s as fellow competitors in the European Cup of Bakery or Coupe d' Europe de la Boulangerie. We have been friends all these years, and we regularly meet as we work, doing demonstrations in Europe, or as jury members at the Coupe du Monde in Paris. This very soft brioche has a soft caramelised cream and sugar mixture in the centre with raspberry pieces. The pastry is masked, dusted and garnished with fresh mint and raspberry.

Strawberry Chocolate Twist

The Strawberry Chocolate Chocolatine Twist made similar to the Coupe Du Monde Chocolatine recipe page 125, but with strawberry chocolate home-made bars. There is a video in other resources on how to make the bars and form the pastry. The pastry is garnished after cooling and baking with strawberry powder, icing sugar, a red isomalt disc of bubble sugar and a ¼ strawberry brushed with apricot jam.

Nutella Cruffin Style Pastry

The Cruffin was originally created by Kate Reid of Lune Croissanterie in Melbourne, Australia in 2013 . A Cruffin is a hybrid of a croissant and muffin. Cruffin style pastries are popular and easily made from croissant pastry page 51, to make them extra crunchy, the pastry block is opened out before sheeting, dredged with sugar, refolded, sheeted to 4 mm and cut into strips of approx. 3cm wide and 25cm long. In the resources section, you can see how I form the pastry and place them into high steel rings to proof and bake. Just before baking and after proofing, I dredge with castor sugar using a small sieve to help caramelise the pastry more during the bake. After baking, they are cooled, filled with Nutella and garnished with a light dust of icing sugar. The steel ring sizes I used were 60mm high and 70mm across. You can use a range of jams, curds, custards, ganache's and other fillings to make a beautiful selection of these pastries.

Home bakers sheeting hack

Many home bakers struggle with rolling pastry evenly when they first make the laminated pastry by hand. If the pastry is rolled unevenly, it follows that the pastry will be of different heights/thicknesses, the underlying layers suffer, causing lack of volume, poor internal texture and misshaped baked pastries. Also, if the pastry is thick on one side and thin on the other, the thin side will colour more rapidly in the oven than the thick side and may burn, ruining the product. A nifty hack is to use rulers, or wooden batons/lats, which can be purchased at your local hardware store. They come in numerous thicknesses and can be cut to size for you in many stores which offer wood cutting services. I would recommend two sizes to start, 3.5mm and 4mm.

Additionally, you need a long rolling pin which extends well beyond the width of the pastry and the wooden guides. I have made a YouTube video on rolling the pastry with the wooden guides, and I have inserted the link below. I hope you find it useful.

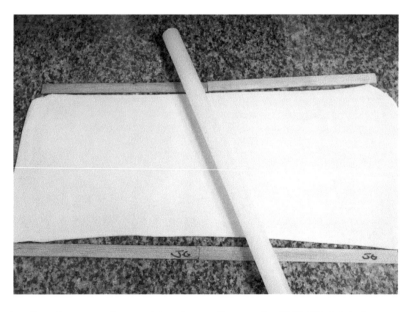

Hand lamination hack using wooden guides https://youtu.be/fyRCB4G4-Qo

Appendix - A – materials and methods

Materials and methods

Optional raw materials used in the process

Spelt croissant dough	Spelt chocolate dough
➢ Spelt flour	Spelt flour
➢ Fresh full fat milk	Fresh full fat milk
➢ Filtered water	Filtered water
➢ Castor sugar	Castor sugar
➢ Skimmed milk powder	Skimmed milk powder
➢ Osmotolerant yeast	Osmotolerant yeast
➢ Barley malt liquid	Barley malt liquid
➢ Salt	Salt
➢ Butter Kerrygold	Butter Kerrygold
➢ Butter dry	Butter dry

Spelt croissant dough

- ➢ Spelt flour
- ➢ Fresh full fat milk
- ➢ Filtered water
- ➢ Castor sugar
- ➢ Skimmed milk powder
- ➢ Osmotolerant yeast
- ➢ Barley malt liquid
- ➢ Salt
- ➢ Butter Kerrygold
- ➢ Butter dry

Spelt chocolate dough

Spelt flour

Fresh full fat milk

Filtered water

Castor sugar

Skimmed milk powder

Osmotolerant yeast

Barley malt liquid

Salt

Butter Kerrygold

Butter dry

- ➢ **Additional ingredients, garnishes and fillings:**
- ➢ Cocoa powder
- ➢ Croissant chocolate bars
- ➢ Candied orange segments
- ➢ Candied orange batons

Details of many ingredient product specifications and a list of their suppliers can be below

The equipment, small tools and other items required in the pastry kitchen

Sample equipment list for Bread and pastry making

1. Wedderburn DS-575 digital weighing scales, with current calibration certificate accurate 16kg to 2g and stainless-steel ingredient bowls for scaling the ingredients.

2. Alla France® calibrated digital infrared thermometer- temperature range – 50 to + 380˚C for measuring dough water and pastry temperature.

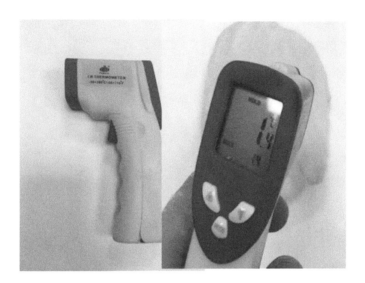

3. Dough mixer – Hobart – 20qt with dough hook and beater attachment

4. Ram pastry sheeter for rolling and sheeting pastry and a water spray bottle for merging pastry

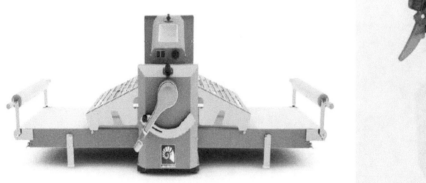 

5. Freezer & refrigerator fitted with shelving space

6. High-speed blast freezer or Cryopack® ice blankets

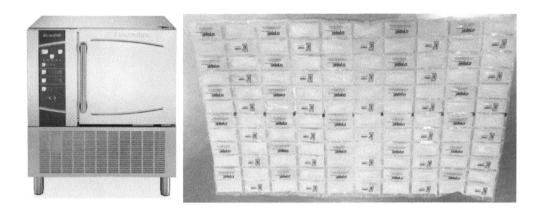

7. Aluminium trays and silicone lining paper for the pastry, used in the freezer, proofing cabinet and oven

8. Makeup and cutting table with refrigerated under storage – stainless steel - Inox

9. Proofing Cabinet capable of maintaining 75-85% humidity and capable of consistently maintaining **25-28°C** (this is <u>a critical</u> maximum temperature) as the butter will run out of the layers if the cabinet gets any hotter.

10. Sveba Dahlen Rack oven and electric Deck oven, Sveba Dalen/Tom Chandley.

11. Cooling Wires

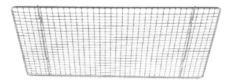

Ingredient storage

> Stainless steel shelving and plastic food grade containers for storing flour, salt, cocoa, sugar, chocolate bars, orange pieces and all dry ambient ingredients.

> Walk-in or reach-in fridge for butter, milk and dough storage to include shelving

Weighing station

> Weighing station table

> Recipe book holder if available

> Ingredient holders and dispensers for salt, milk powder, sugar, spelt flour, cocoa, and other items.

> Digital weighing scales x 1-16 kg capacity precision 1g

> Scoops x 6

> Jug 1 x 1L; Jug 1 x 2L

> Flour Sieve

Mixing station

> Digital infrared thermometer for measuring dough temperature

> Hobart mixer 10qt capacity with a dough hook

Dough storage containers

> Plastic dough containers and stainless-steel racks

Lamination station

> Pastry sheeter free standing-1150cm x 60 cm pastry belts

> Large rolling pin x 1; Small rolling pin x 1

> Measuring tape / ruler / templates

> Water spray gun

Makeup table and small tools

Small tools for pastry making:

- Four-wheel pastry dividers x 1
- French knife-25cm; Trimming knife-10cm
- Bench scraper
- Plastic scraper
- Pastry brush
- Digital weighing scales x 1 - Capacity 6kg - precision 1g

Trollies and baking trays

- 30 x 18" baking trays; 15 x 18" baking trays
- 16-space stainless steel rack

Freezing equipment

- Domestic freezer
- Chest freezer
- Upright freezer
- Walk-in freezer
- Blast freezer if available
- Ice blankets

Packaging station for sales and distribution

- ➢ Racking for storage of wrapping and packaging equipment

- ➢ Paper bags for 1-2 units

- ➢ Cardboard packaging boxes, for 1, 4- & 6-units ambient sale

- ➢ Cardboard boxes 35cm x 45cm for wholesale sales of 50 frozen units

- ➢ Plastic liners for cardboard boxes

- ➢ Packaging tape dispensers

- ➢ Product label blanks

- ➢ PC station for label printing of products

Materials and methods

Spelt *(Triticum spelta)* Flour:

Appearance: Fine powder/quality cereals

Odour: Free from mustiness and foreign odours

Taste: Mildly nutty flavour free from any rancidity

Additives: If required the flour or cereal is to be produced in accordance with relevant legislation

Raw flour product to be acceptable under Irish legislation specifically; The Bread & Flour Regulation 1998 & Amendments

Storage: 3 months for wholemeal stone ground

Storage: 6 months for white spelt flour

Source: http://www.vvrsaustralia.com.au/wp-content/uploads/2013/02/Spelt-flour-300x224.jpg

Spelt can be used as the main ingredient in the croissant recipes, when the liquid component is added to the spelt flour and mixed, two proteins which are naturally occurring in the flour absorb water and swell; this is known as hydrating the flour. The two proteins, gliadin and glutenin, combine in the dough when hydrated to form the protein called gluten (The Baking Industry Research Trust, 2016). The gluten gives the dough the properties it requires to form an elastic matrix which can trap the CO_2 gases given off as a by-product of yeast fermentation. The trapped gases and the elastic protein matrix are responsible for the light, airy structure of the crumb of yeasted baked goods.

Whole milk:

Total solids (% m/m) Min 12.0% Milk
Butterfat (% m/m) 3.5 – 4.0%
MSNF (% m/m) 8.5 -9.0 %
Specific Gravity min 1.030
Phosphatase (p-nitro phenol) <10ug/ml <10ug/ml
Antibiotics negative
pH 6.7 ± 0.2 6.7 ± 0.2
Appearance Free from burn particles, foreign and extraneous matter
Colour creamy white Free from chemicals and other flavours. Clean milk flavour. Temperature (°C) Less than °1C max 6°C

Source: http://strathroy.lairdev.com/wp-content/uploads/2011/11/goats_milk_01.jpg

Milk is one of the moistening and enriching agents used to make the spelt dough, water being the other. It contributes towards a softer eating product and the natural sugar present in the milk improve crust colour.

Castor or granulated sugar:

Food grade: Free from contamination, mould growth or microbial spoilage
Appearance: White crystallised granules free from clumps or damp
Colour: Shiny with a highly reflective surface; free from impurities
Flavour: Tastes sweet of sugar with a rich flavour
Aroma -N/A
Storage; Store in a cool dry place away from contaminants in a sealed container
Shelf life: Indefinite (Best before end date usually three years after packaging)
Variety: Gem

Source: http://www.conatycatering.com/image/cache/data/01105506-500x500.jpg

Sugar contributes sweetness and enrichment to the dough. Sugar is also a food source for the yeast and assists the yeast, by feeding it, to operate in a high-fat environment. Sugar contributes towards a softer eating product, imparts sweetness and has a significant role in the colour of the pastry during the baking process.

Milk powder:

Manufactured from fresh pasteurized milk. A white to slightly yellowish, free flowing powder. Taste is clean slightly sweet, milky and neutral with no distinctive off-flavours. No neutralising materials, additives or preservatives product packed in multiwall Kraft paper bag with poly liner can be stored in dry cool conditions (below 25°C and 70 % Rh) for 1 year.

Source: https://kerrygold.com/products/kerrygold-full-cream-milk-powder/

Milk powder improves both crumb and crust colour in the dough and contributes towards a softer eating baked product.

Barley liquid malt:

Appearance: A viscous liquid amber or yellowish brown in colour (Free from any adulterants, off odour, foreign flavour and impurities)
Identification: Positive for Carbohydrates
Taste: Characteristic Malt and sweet taste free from any detectable foreign or off flavour i.e. not be sharp or bitter or sour tail

Source: https://www.meridianfoods.co.uk/Products/Other-ranges/Natural-Sweeteners/Organic/Organic-Barley-Malt-Extract

Non-diastatic malt contributes towards the rich chestnut colour of the pastry and is also a food source for the yeast, maintaining dough stability during the cold fermentation process.

Compressed yeast:

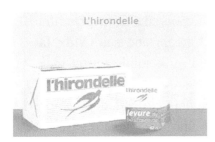

Supplier: Lesaffre
Group: Baker's yeast L'hirondelle (Swift)
Pack Size: 10kg 10x500g
Pack Type: Box
Product Form: Solid
Product Colour: Grey
Shelf life 35 days when stored at 1 °C-4°C

Source: https://lesaffre.uk/products/compressed-yeast/

Baker's yeast or Saccharomyces cerevisiae is the biological raising agent used to provide raising of the pastry. The by-product of yeast fermentation - CO_2 is trapped by the gluten matrix and coupled with the mechanical lamination of the butter layers in the dough, provide the pastry with its light and airy structure as the gas expands, trapped by the gluten matrix in the oven during baking causing the pastry to rise

Salt:

Iodized Salt is dried, sieved, edible and iodized for human consumption
Sodium chloride as NaCl: minimum 97.0 % (on dry matter)
Moisture content: max 3.0% (m/m)
Water insoluble matter: max 0.2 % (m/m)
Iodine: 30.0 – 50.0 mg/kg (means 50 – 84mg of potassium iodate per kg of salt)
Colour: shall be white and 10g of salt in 100ml water shall give a colourless solution having a neutral reaction. Store under dry, ventilated and hygienic conditions

Source: http://fyi.uwex.edu/safepreserving/files/2014/08/salt.jpg

Salt has an astringent effect on the gluten formed in the dough. Salt also helps to control the fermentation of the yeast and imparts colour to the finished baked dough.

Butter:

Food grade: free from contamination, rancidity, mould growth or microbial spoilage. Sourced from grass-fed cows. Made with pasteurized cream and salt. Milk fat 80% moisture max. 18.2% and milk solid non-fat max. 1.8%, No trans-fat, No hormones
No artificial colours or ingredients No added vegetable oil. Butter has a shelf life of around 3 months for unsalted and 5 months for salted butter. Keep refrigerated at +3°C.

Source: http://kerrygold.com/images/sized/images/uploads/KG_Pure_Irish_Butter-604x414.png

Butter enriches the croissant dough, the natural beta carotene adding colour to both the crust and the crumb. Butter shortens the dough and imparts both flavour and colour to the overall dough. This butter also lubricates the gluten and is added to the dough at the mixing stage for this purpose.

Dry butter:

Food grade: free from contamination, rancidity, mould growth or microbial spoilage
Pasteurised cream (manufactured from cow milk), lactic ferments
Milk fat 84%, moisture max. 14.6% and milk solid non-fat max. 1.8%. No colour or additives
Butter has a shelf life of around 3 months for unsalted and 5 months for salted butter.
Keep refrigerated at + 3 - 8°C max

Source: https://pro.elle-et-vire.com/en/products/butters/extra-dry-butter-84-fat

Butter enriches the croissant dough, the natural beta carotene adding colour to both the crust and the crumb. Butter shortens the dough and imparts both flavour and colour to the overall dough. This butter is also drier than the Kerrygold butter used in the dough making and is specially designed for the lamination process. The lamination butter is rolled and folded into the dough, building up tiny alternating and layers of dough and butter. The butter separates the dough as it is folded generating an independent film which enables these alternating layers of dough and butter to form. The lamination is the building block of the pastry and is referred to as mechanical aeration, it is the second of two types of aeration used to achieve aeration in the pastry and imparts a light, flaky property to the finished pastry.

Cocoa powder:

Food grade: free from contamination, rancidity, mould growth or microbial spoilage
Appearance: Dry fine brown powder free from clumps (Very similar to heavy cornflour)
Colour: Dark brown with an unreflective appearance; free from impurities
Flavour: Tastes of chocolate however has a tendency to be more astringent and bitter
Aroma – Chocolate aroma
Storage; Store in a cool dry place away from contaminants in a sealed container
Shelf life: Indefinite (Best before end date usually three years after packaging)
Sole Producer; Barry Callebaut (Produced under licence)
Other Notes; Free from dairy (Lactose)

Source: http://foodie-isms.com/wp-content/uploads/2011/04/cocoa-powder.jpg

Cocoa powder is used to provide colour and flavour to the dough using a natural product. In this instance, the cocoa powder is mixed with the laminating butter in advance of the laminating process; a butter block is made and incorporated into the dough. When used in this fashion, the chocolate butter not only provides flavour and colour, it also gives the pastry a unique aspect or look, differentiating it from other products in this class of pastry.

Cocoa as a functional ingredient in chocolate laminating dough

Chocolate croissant batons:

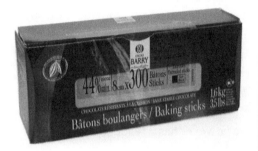

300 pieces Cardboard carton // 15 Cardboard cartons per case
Cacao Barry
Comments: Easy, fast, and formulated to be baked. For filling Viennese pastry like pain au chocolat.
Specifications,
Storage Conditions: Dry and cool (68- 72°F, 20- 22°C)
Shelf Life (months):12.0
Ingredients: Sugar, cocoa liquor, cocoa butter, emulsifier: soya lecithin, vanillin flavour
Additional Notes: Sugar: 54% Cocoa mass: 44% Store in a dry place, away from foreign odours and protected from direct sunlight.

Source: https://www.cacao-barry.com/en-CA/chocolate-couverture-cocoa/chd-bb-308by/extruded-batons-boulangers

The chocolate bars for making pain au chocolat are specially made and tempered chocolate pieces which are specifically designed not to burn in the oven when subjected to heat. Their primary function is the provision of flavour in the product.

Candied orange segments

A firm, whole candied orange slice with a punchy citrus flavour combined with a natural sweet structure. Perfect for enrobing with chocolate. A natural product without sulphites.
Storage Conditions: Dry and cool (68- 72°F, 20-22°C). Shelf Life (months):18.0
Store in a dry place, away from foreign odours and protected from direct sunlight.

Source: https://www.keylink.org/product/candied-orange-slices-drained

The candied orange segments are a garnish designed to reflect the flavour of the product. The candied orange segments are added after baking and cooling for decorative purposes. They are a natural product free of sulphides.

Candied orange batons:

Premium candied orange strips are dark and firm with an intense orange aroma which can be enrobed or dipped in chocolate. A natural product without sulphites.
Storage Conditions: Dry and cool (68- 72°F, 20- 22°C). Shelf Life 18 months.
Store in a dry place, away from foreign odours and protected from direct sunlight.

Source: https://www.keylink.org/product/candied-straight-orange-peel-strips-drained-1

The candied orange bars are a filling designed to enhance the flavour of the product. The candied orange segments are added before baking for flavouring purposes. They are a natural product, free of sulphides.

Appendix - B – Pre fermented Croissant dough hand lamination

Hand laminated croissant 50% preferment & sourdough levain

Hand Laminated Croissant 50% Preferment + Levain

Ingredients	1 MIX	1/2 mix	Based on flour 100% Bakers %	Hydration %
	g	g	767	55.11
Preferment Stage 1 Overnight 14-16 hrs				
Strong Flour	368	184	48.0 %	
Water	205	103	26.7 %	
Yeast	0.5	0.25	0.1 %	
Total	574		74.8 %	
Sourdough addition dough stage day 1				
Water	30	15	3.9 %	
Flour	30	15	3.9 %	
Sourdough	15	8	2.0 %	
Sourdough starter 1 : 2 : 2	75	38	9.8 %	
Dough Stage day 2				
Preferment stage	574	287	74.8 %	
Sourdough stage	75	38	9.8 %	
Strong Flour	368	184	48.0 %	
Milk	180	90	23.5 %	
Sugar	96	48	12.5 %	
Yeast fresh	29	15	3.8 %	
Milk powder	18	9	2.3 %	
Barley malt extract (non diastatic)	15	8	2.0 %	
Salt	13	7	1.7 %	
Butter	38	19	5.0 %	

	1 MIX	1/2 mix	Butter on Dough %	Total Butter % in both Dough & Lamination
Dough head weight	1,331	665		
Lamination Stage				
Laminating butter	335	168	25.2	30.1
Total batch weight	1,666	833		
Yield	22	11		
Scaling wt in grams	75			

I regularly engage with international bakers of all levels of proficiency in online platforms such as Facebook and Instagram, assisting them with problems and trying to help them achieve improved results in laminated pastry making. One of the most consistent problems or issues I identified from these platforms were those who hand-laminated at home and at work. Pastry elastic recoil presented problems for many while hand rolling; so, to address this, I have formulated a special new recipe, which I have test baked several times, adjusting the preferment, hydration and the work sequence. The result is a very pleasant tasting pastry, which hand rolls extremely well due to the doughs' increased hydration and overnight pre fermentation and additional sourdough.

The flour used by bakers in different countries varies greatly. In Canada for example, patent flour can be very strong with protein levels typically 10.0 – 12.5% (12.8 – 14.5% dry basis) and an ash content of : 0.35 – 0.55% (0.41 – 0.64 dry basis). My Canadian friend and colleague Alan Dumonceaux, (CDM) and world masters Viennoiserie candidate was recommending a pre fermented technique for those who only had very strong flour available to them. This process is a two-day process, where, day 1; a preferment is made, the sourdough is added, and the dough is fermented overnight at room temperature 18-22°C. Day 2, the preferment is mixed into a dough along with the remaining 50% of the flour and the rest of the ingredients. The dough was mixed by me using a Kitchen Aid stand mixer for 3 minutes on slow, and three minutes on medium speed using a dough hook. The dough is fermented at room temperature for 45 minutes, then de gassed, by rolling out using a rolling pin into a rectangle, placed on a tray, covered with plastic and chilled for 2 hours in a fridge until the dough is at 3-4°C. The butter block should be prepared at this time and placed in the fridge until required.

The dough is then taken from the fridge along with the butter block. I used the 3-4-3 system for croissant and the 3-4-4 system for pain au chocolat. The lock-in is performed and it is possible to give the dough all its turns together, providing the room and surfaces you work on are relatively cool. In warm climates, I recommend that the make-up is staggered, placing the pastry back to chill for 30m min in a fridge or freezer until cool enough to work. The pastry may need a little bit extra dusting flour when processing. When all the turns are completed and the pastry is ready to process, sheet as normal, cut, shape and proof. The pastry will be quite active, and I noticed that the croissants and pain au chocolat will proof quicker than normal.

The science behind this method is to make an overnight preferment using 50% of the flour in the recipe and let the enzymes do most of the work on the gluten during fermentation. As many of the bakers online also bake sourdough, I added just under 10% sourdough to the recipe; adding extra flavour and extensibility to the dough. The protease degrades the protein overnight during the fermentation process, which greatly improves extensibility and makes the dough a pleasure to roll. I have made the recipe with up to 57% hydration (using a 13% extra strong bakers' flour), but I found that the wetter dough required a lot more dusting flour and was quite sticky and not too easy to handle. My recommendation is to use approx.. 55% hydration. Have fun everyone,

Jimmy G.

Other online resources

My YouTube Channel https://www.youtube.com/channel/ucsmfbyjsiu4e7du-kmu6ing/

Twisted chocolatine shaping using homemade chocolate bars https://youtu.be/klsvyc1omoo

Pain chocolate shaping - Three ways https://youtu.be/uheq8fjbffk

Croissant bicolor 3-4-4 pastry process https://youtu.be/q-o0cyjane0

Twisted chocolatine bicolor shaping and makeup https://youtu.be/qr_SS3aWSRs

Slicing laminated pastry to relieve elastic recoil https://youtu.be/gscqic8hpxk

Croissant make up dough video with rolling and a 3 fold https://youtu.be/nhsavshz6c0

Explaining elastic recoil tension in laminated pastry https://youtu.be/vi90mhc2t_U

The lock in process of dough and butter in pastry making https://youtu.be/J_j4umea7ow

Butter block and hand lamination https://youtu.be/KI7VTQQISFw

Coupe du Monde Chocolatine Toulouse, France 2019 https://youtu.be/HQW4TfDnmvY

Chocolatine scored using a claw and scored using a knife https://youtu.be/s-aV1bzKnpc

Raspberry pear marinade, dusting and masking techniques https://youtu.be/qYUHmcZbypU

How to incorporate trimmings to reduce wastage https://youtu.be/mA22qWphP8E

The correct procedure for wrapping laminated pastry https://youtu.be/RAb-aVWX6tQ

Making frozen Crème Pâtissière pieces for viennoiserie https://youtu.be/kwUZEcjtak4

How to insert frozen Crème Pâtissière into proofed pastry https://youtu.be/NBm1Ti-YAWU

Christmas jiggle jiggle https://youtu.be/2ifa63fspqs

Christmas chocolatines https://youtu.be/bxzinvf118e

Seaweed dissertation: https://arrow.tudublin.ie/tfschcafdis/1/

Cruffin style pastries: https://youtu.be/yturuzkkmdc

5-4-3 Hand lamination sourdough croissant pastry: https://youtu.be/irmbjlvxls4

Chilling laminated dough using frozen vegetables https://youtu.be/-WZ9w0gPjyg

Brød &Taylor home proofer: https://brodandtaylor.com/

Hand lamination hack using wooden guides https://youtu.be/fyRCB4G4-Qo

Kouign Amman preparation final fold https://www.youtube.com/watch?v=gNM22D7jLhY

References

Arat, E. 2019. *The History of Turkish Coffee.* https://www.turkishcoffeeworld.com/History-of-Coffee-s/60.htm, last access 2019-11-19.

Bramen, L. 2010. *When Food Changed History: The French Revolution.* Https://www.smithsonianmag.com/arts-culture/when-food-canged-history-the-french-revolution-93598442/, last access 2019-11-19.

Chevallier, J. 2009. *August Zang and the French Croissant: How Viennoiserie came to France.* 2nd ed. North Hollywood (California), Chez Jim Books.

Culinary Institute of America. 2016. *Baking and Pastry.* Hoboken (New Jersey), John Wiley & Sons.

City of Vienna, 2019. *1683 - the beginning of Viennese coffee house culture.* Https://www.wien.gv.at/english/culture-history/viennese-coffee-culture.html, last access 2019-11-19.].

Fiegl, A. 2015. *Is the Croissant really French - A brief history of the croissant – from kipfel to Cronut?* Https://www.smithsonianmag.com/arts-culture/croissant-really-french-180955130/, last access 2019-11-19.

Goldstein D, Mintz S. 2015. *The Oxford Companion to Sugar and Sweets.* Oxford, Oxford University Press.

Hartings, M. 2016. *Chemistry in Your Kitchen.* Cambridge, The Royal Society of Chemistry.

Labensky SR, Martel P, Van Damme E. 2009. *On Baking.* 2nd ed. Columbus (Ohio), Pearson Prentice Hall.

NIIR Board of Consultants & Engineers. 2014. *The Complete Technology Book on Bakery Products (Baking Science with formulation and production).* 3rd ed. Deli, NIIR Project Consultancy Services.

Pastry Chef Central. 2019. *Puff Pastry Dough.* https://www.pastrychef.com/Puff-Pastry-Dough_ep_70.html, last access 2019-11-19.

Peterson, J. 2012. *Baking.* Berkeley (California), Potter/tenspeed/Harmony.

Willan, A. 2016. *Oxford Reference: France.* Http://www.oxfordreference.com/view/10.1093/acref/9780199313396.001.0001/acref-9780199313396-e-202 last access 2019-11-19.

BakerPedia, 2020. *Croissant.* [Online]
Available at: https://bakerpedia.com/processes/croissant/
[Accessed 8 April 2020].

Bakerpedia, n.d. *Puff Pastry.* [Online]
Available at: https://bakerpedia.com/processes/puff-pastry/
[Accessed 8 April 2020].

Berry, D. R., Russell, I. & Stewart, G., 2012. *Yeast Biotechnology.* 3 ed. NY(NY): Springer.

Brown, A. C., 2018. *Understanding food : principles and preparation.* 6th ed. Manoa(Hawaii): Cengage Learning.

Calvel, R. 2001. *The Taste of Bread.* s.l.:Springer.

Cauvain, S. P. 2017. *Baking Problems Solved.* 1 ed. Cambridge: Woodhead Publishing.

Chevallier, J. 2009. *August Zang and the French Croissant: How Viennoiserie Came to France.* 2nd ed. Northwood(California): Chez Jim Books.

Doves Farm, 2020. *European flour numbering system.* [Online]
Available at: https://www.dovesfarm.co.uk/hints-tips/cheat-sheets/european-flour-numbering-system
[Accessed 17 May 2020].

Goldstein, D. & Mintz, S., 2015. *The Oxford Companion to Sugar and Sweets.* Oxford: Oxford University Press.

Griffin, J. 2016. *Chocolatine Time-lapse Video YouTube,* Galway: s.n.

Griffin, J. A. 2015. *An Investigative study into the beneficial use of seaweed in bread and the broader food industry.* Dublin: James A. Griffin.

Griffin, J. A. 2015. *One-minute croissant butter block technique,* Galway: James Griffin.

Griffin, J. A. 2016. *Pain au Chocolat "Wobble" Test ,* Galway: James Griffin.

Haegens, N. n.d. *Puff pastry and Danish pastry.* [Online]
Available at: http://www.classofoods.com/page4_1.html
[Accessed 08 April 2020].

Hutkins, R. 2008. *Microbiology and Technology of Fermented Foods.* Hoboken(New Jersey): John Wiley & Sons.

Jason Davies, 2020. *jasondavies.com.* [Online]
Available at: https://www.jasondavies.com/wordcloud/
[Accessed 20 March 2020].

Labensky, S. R., Martel, P. & Van Damme, E., 2009. *On Baking.* 2nd ed. Columbus(Ohio): Pearson Prentice Hall.

Lonely Planet Food, 2017. *From the Source - France: Authentic Recipes From the People That Know Them ....* 1 ed. Wilson(Wyoming): Lonely Planet Food.

NIIR Board of Consultants and Engineers, 2014. *The Complete Technology Book on Bakery Products (Baking Science with formulation and production).* 3rd ed. Deli: Niir Project Consultancy Services.

Ranken, M., Baker, C. G. .. & Kill, R. eds., 1997. *Food Industries Manual.* 24 ed. Padstow(Cornwall): Springer.

Rodriguez, B. M. & Merangioni, A. G., 2018. *Physics Today,* 1(70), p. 71.

Rondo, n.d. *Rondo Dough-how and more,* Burgdorf: s.n.

Stamm, M. 2011. *The Pastry Chef's Apprentice: An Insider's Guide to Creating and Baking Sweet confections and pastries taught by the masters.* Beverly(MA): Quarry Books.

The Baking Industry Research Trust, 2016. *WHAT ROLE DOES GLUTEN PLAY IN BREAD MAKING?.* [Online]
Available at: http://www.bakeinfo.co.nz/Facts/Gluten/What-role-does-gluten-play-in-bread-making-
[Accessed 1 May 2016].

The Culinary Institute of America, 2016. *Baking and Pastry.* Hoboken(New Jersey): John Wiley & Sons.

Vernet, S., 2020. *French Croissants,* Montpellier: s.n.

Weekendbakery.com, 2020. *Understanding flour types.* [Online]
Available at: https://www.weekendbakery.com/posts/understanding-flour-types/
[Accessed 17 May 2020].

Willan, A., 2016. *Oxford Reference: France.* [Online]
Available at:
http://www.oxfordreference.com/view/10.1093/acref/9780199313396.001.0001/acref-

9780199313396-e-202
[Accessed 16 January 2016].

Yankellow, J., 2005. *Lamination: Layers beyond imagination,* San Francisco: s.n.

Index

L - #0021 - 210720 - C189 - 279/216/10 [12] - CB - DID2873435